MILLARD FULLER

BEYOND THE AMERICAN DREAM

D0921057

Smyth & Helwys Publishing, Inc.
6316 Peake Road
Macon, Georgia 31210-3960
1-800-747-3016
©2010 by Smyth & Helwys Publishing
All rights reserved.
Printed in the United States of America.

The paper used in this publication meets the minimum requirements of
American National Standard for Information Sciences—
Permanence of Paper for Printed Library Materials.
ANSI Z39.48–1984. (alk. paper)

Library of Congress Cataloging-in-Publication Data

Fuller, Millard, 1935–2009.
Beyond the American dream / by Millard D. Fuller.
p. cm.
Includes bibliographical references and index.
ISBN 978-1-57312-563-5 (pbk. : alk. paper)
1. Fuller, Millard, 1935-2009.
2. Habitat for Humanity International, inc.—History.
3. Poor—Services for—United States.
4. Poor—Services for.
5. American Dream.
I. Title.
HV97.H32F315 2010
362.5'83—dc22

2010030542

Dedication by Linda Fuller

To Naomi Grace Luedi, born September 18, 2008.
Millard dedicated his last three books to our other
grandchildren, so it seems appropriate to have this
book, actually the first one he wrote, dedicated to
our most recent grandchild—the fifth child of
Georgia and Manfred Luedi.

Contents

Preface

By Linda Caldwell Fuller

When Millard left business at age thirty and turned his life in a new direction, he began writing an autobiography. He had started journaling as a student in his early twenties. Then, after leaving law school, he became more diligent about making daily entries. He kept his journal in his desk and wrote in great detail about his business and law ventures. Millard's eight-year journey from pauper to millionaire could be a book of its own. Realizing this, he began to compile and edit his entries into manuscript form.

In 1968, just as we were moving to Koinonia, Millard completed the rough draft of the manuscript and mailed it to a publisher he knew. It was returned within a few weeks "to be considered at a later time" (postmarked October 20, 1970) and remained in that manila envelope for forty years. Now and then, as we moved house or cleaned shelves, I asked Millard if it was about time we got the book published. He would basically brush it off. "Not now. I'm too busy."

Millard used to tell people that he was "a poor millionaire" because his part of the business had amounted to only one million dollars. However, one must keep in mind that a million dollars in 1965 was worth *much* more than it is today. Inflation between 1935 and 2009 is significant. Consider the cost of postage. In 1965, sending a first-class letter cost five cents. As this book goes to press, the cost is forty-four cents—nearly nine times as much!

Millard's first thirty years (1935–1965) cover interesting transitions in history: the post-Great Depression era, World War II, the Industrial Revolution, the beginning of the civil rights movement, the first commercial trans-Atlantic flights, the first moon landing, the Cuban crisis, electric typewriters, Elvis Presley, the Beatles, the assassinations of President John F. Kennedy and Martin Luther King, Jr., Woodstock, Vietnam War, and Peace Niks.

One of Millard's favorite movies was *Back to the Future* (Universal Pictures, 1985). In a real sense, I believe that this book is indeed a journey "back to the future." It is clear to me that God had his hand in making and using this man in extraordinary ways. As *Beyond the American Dream* goes to press, there is a documentary in production that will also portray Millard's incredible journey.

Millard's mother, Estin, died in 1938 when he was three years old. I was told that she started having severe abdominal pains one morning and died that night. Three years later, his father, Render, remarried and had two sons, Nick and Doyle. Millard's stepmother, Eunice, and Render were married for twenty-seven years before she passed away in December 1968, a few months after we moved from New Jersey to Koinonia in Georgia. Millard's father died four years later as we were making preparations to become missionaries in Africa.

By the time Millard finished the manuscript in 1968, we had three children: Christopher, born in Lawton, Oklahoma, in 1960; Estin Kimberly, born in Montgomery, Alabama, in 1962; and Linda Faith, born in Glen Ridge, New Jersey, in 1967. Our fourth child, Georgia, was born in 1971 when we lived at Koinonia Farm near Americus, Georgia.

I believe Millard intended to focus on his various church, academic, political, and business pursuits when writing this book. This could be why he does not include much detail about his upbringing and our family. I have taken the liberty of including a few vignettes throughout the book from my perspective to help fill out his story.

Working on this book presented me with opportunities to relish and share precious memories found in photographs. I had hundreds from which to choose. The most difficult part was narrowing down my selections. Kelli Yoder, a dedicated Fuller Center staff member, made my work easier by scanning old photographs and copying others from archive files.

I wish to acknowledge our four children, who encouraged me to publish their father's first book. They read part or all of the manuscript as soon as I had created computer documents of it. They were eager to know more about their father's early years and were amazed at the stories. This was their father's only autobiography, a genuine treasure for them, for their children, and for generations to come.

My friends, both far and near, went over and beyond with prayers and other kinds of support when Millard passed away suddenly and unexpectedly in February 2009. Their love continues. At times, I have had to ask family and friends to bear with me when it was necessary to go "underground" for a time to meet deadlines. It would be inmpossible to give proper recognition and express adequate appreciation for the kindnesses showered on me.

Among my friends are those who wrote the foreword and afterword. Ronnie McBrayer knew Millard well. He had preached in Ronnie's church in Santa Rosa Beach, Florida. Soon after Millard died, Ronnie preached a sermon about Millard's life and ministry. It deeply touched my family and me. I remembered that sermon when I began working on this book and thought including it would be a perfect fit. I thank Ronnie for doing the honors.

As for the Afterword, I must mention that it was as amusing as it was embarrassing for Millard and me to cross paths with our longtime friend Tony Campolo in an airport. Without fail, he always pointed to Millard and began shouting, "Hey, everybody, here's Millard Fuller! He started Habitat for Humanity, and you need to get to know this guy." After repeating this several times, he would offer warm hugs, good laughs, and as much visiting as possible before we had to say goodbye and run to our gates. When we were planning Millard's memorial service to be held six weeks after his death, Tony was the first person I thought of as the key speaker. I phoned him. He looked at his calendar. He would be on a speaking trip in Hawaii with plans to continue to New Zealand. He said he would call me back. A few hours later, he agreed to do it by cutting his engagement one day short and taking a redeye flight to Atlanta and then on to Auckland, New Zealand, at the conclusion of the service. Tony's wife, Peggy, and I have been close friends for many years. Due to the fact that both of us were fortunate enough to have type A, world-traveling husbands, we had much in common. My profound gratitude goes out to both Tony and Peggy.

Lastly, but certainly not least, I express appreciation for the pleasure of working with our dear friends at Smyth & Helwys Publishing. Millard began working with this publishing house when he wrote *Theology of the Hammer* in 1994. They also published his *Building Materials for Life*, a three-part series, in recent years. Each publication was more of a "handshake" than a complicated web of contracts. There was a friendship and trust that went both ways. When I got in touch with publisher Lex Horton, he didn't hesitate after glancing at the manuscript. He gave me the "green light," and it was a joy working with him, editor Leslie Andres, and their colleagues every step of the way.

In conclusion, I want everyone to know what a blessed woman I am to have known Millard Fuller and been his wife, friend, and partner for an awesome fifty years. My faith assures me that Millard and I will be reunited one day. I am proud to be the mother of our four children and ten grandchildren (Angelia Rose Luedi, an anencephalic baby, died a few minutes after birth). I have meaningful work to do in staying healthy, keeping my house in order, and trying to fulfill God's calling on our lives to eradicate poverty housing in the world. That's a tall order, but I believe it makes me one of the richest people on Earth. For all of this, I am blessed far beyond the American dream.

Foreword

By Ronnie McBrayer

He was the author of ten books and awarded more than a dozen honorary doctorate degrees. He was a millionaire before age thirty and gave away his entire fortune before he was forty. He was a lawyer, a friend to presidents and world leaders, an advocate for the poor, and a recipient of the Presidential Medal of Freedom. He was a husband, father, and grandfather. He was a tall, skinny kid with big ears from Lanett, Alabama.

He was exceptionally kind to those he had no specific cause to be kind to, including me.

He was founder of Habitat for Humanity and the Fuller Center for Housing, both movements organized to eliminate substandard housing worldwide. In his more than thirty years at the helm of those organizations, a quarter of a million simple, decent, affordable homes were constructed in close to a hundred countries. And because of his unfailing vision and tenacity, he was responsible for sheltering more than a million people who had been living in poverty.

He was Millard Fuller, now buried in the red dirt outside the town of Americus, Georgia. With no marker for his grave, his body rests inside a wooden box at the top of Picnic Hill on Koinonia Farm.

Millard and I became friends years ago when I went to work for the Habitat for Humanity affiliate in Walton County, Florida. In the aftermath of and relief work that followed Hurricane Katrina, he and I began to correspond regularly, and our friendship strengthened. When I jumped into the publishing world with my first book, Millard helped show me the way and wrote my first endorsement. I'd like to say that I offered something to Millard in our friendship, but that's not true. Like everything he ever did, he was the ruthless giver in the relationship, and I received. We all received. The world is a better place for it, and we are all better people.

Just weeks before he died, Millard Fuller spoke to my congregation about his life's work. As was typical, it was one of four presentations he gave that day to four different churches. He gushed that morning with all the zeal and energy of a man half his age, and his words were vintage Millard Fuller. He said,

> When I turned seventy people came to me and said, "You've built housing for a million people. Why don't you take it easy now?" But why would I want to do that? I love what I do. I'm not dead yet. I don't even feel bad. I started Habitat when I was forty. Now I've started the Fuller Center at seventy, and I have to work faster, because I don't have much time left. I've ratcheted up my pace quite a bit because it is a blessing and a privilege to do God's work, to be aggressive doers of good deeds.

Now that Millard has completed his part of God's work, I am certain he finds himself in a curious situation: unemployed. Millard is probably in heaven right now, still in a training program of sorts, learning new skills for whatever is next, because there is no substandard housing in the world where he now lives. In that world, there are no more Asian slums, no more inner-city destitution, no more African squalor, no more Appalachian or Delta hardship, no more of the grinding poverty Millard combated most of his life. For you see, that house in which he now resides is his dream and vision come true. It is a house with many rooms, room enough for all to be warm, safe, fed, and dry. At last, Millard Fuller has reached the place where his work is finally and magnificently no longer needed.

But Millard Fuller was not always the man of self-sacrifice so many of us knew and loved. Before he was thirty, he and his business partner were millionaires. Ingenuity, hard work, limitless energy: these all drove him to greater and greater success. And they also drove his marriage into the ground. In the earlier years of their relationship, his wife of fifty years, Linda Fuller, was raising their young family and enjoying the rewards of her husband's success, but she was alone. Millard was at the office day and night making a fortune, keeping the family in wealth, and all the family really wanted was Millard. Linda left him, and it crushed Millard's spirit.

Millard was never one to take rejection sitting still, and Linda finally agreed for him to join her in New York City. They worked it out. They forgave one another and made the decision that things had to change, and they each had a spiritual awakening. The success, the wealth, the possessions, and the insatiable desire for the next rung on the ladder were stealing their lives away. Millard summed it up best: "We wanted to follow Christ, and we felt that we had to unburden ourselves of all the stuff we had accumulated to make it possible to go wherever God wanted us to go."

They ended up in Americus, Georgia, at a place called Koinonia Farm, where they met a man who would become their mentor, Clarence Jordan. They intended to visit with Clarence for an hour or two. The Fullers stayed for a month. Then, as planned, they went home, gave away everything, and moved to Koinonia Farm.

Koinonia Farm, the place that so shaped the Fullers, was founded by Clarence Jordan in the 1940s, based on his intended goal to "do something for the poor."[1] He implemented a farming community where men and women, blacks and whites, rich and poor lived together under the parenthood of God; where love became the substitute for violence; and where those who lived in residence shared their possessions generously with others. Koinonia was a truly alternative Christian community that served as a "demonstration plot for the kingdom of God."[2]

Clarence understood that those who chose this radical path would be few, but he was okay with that. He often described such people as dynamite in a coil or gasoline compressed by a piston. These were small, constrictive spaces, but it was actually in their smallness that explosive power ignited. Koinonia became a place like that. It was never very large, no more than several dozen people and sometimes down to only the Jordans and a handful of others, but it was explosive in its influence and power. Millard and Linda Fuller were two firebrands that came bursting out of that little slice of the kingdom of God. With Clarence, they birthed the idea that poverty housing could and should be eliminated. Simple, decent, affordable housing could be provided to all if people of faith would foster partnerships with "God's people in need."[3]

The first such partnership homes were built in the early 1970s at Koinonia Farm, and in 1976, Millard and Linda Fuller took the idea worldwide. Every person who has ever volunteered on a Habitat for

Humanity or Fuller Center work project, or given money to sponsor a home or renovation project, is in effect taking the hands of Jordan and the Fullers and continuing their good work.

In the last book Millard Fuller wrote before his death, he said,

> I am often asked where I get the energy to do all that I do . . . . Well, I believe God loves me. . . . I have long been convinced that God put me on this earth for a purpose. . . . I practice good health habits. . . . I am careful to get adequate rest and to eat properly. . . . I like to laugh . . . and I have been blessed with a wonderful life mate. . . . All of this, I think, contributes to my energy. How long will it last? Who knows? But as long as my energy lasts and as long as I am blessed with a good mind, I intend to stay at it."[4]

And stay at it he did, until God quickly and unexpectedly called him Home.

In addition to being Millard's mentor, Clarence Jordan is best known for writing the *Cotton Patch Gospel*, printed after his death. It is a translation of the Greek New Testament into the vernacular and times of South Georgia in the 1960s. It was not intended for scholars and seminary students, but as a prophetic work speaking to his times. A portion of his translation from 2 Corinthians could apply as a benediction to Millard's life, so well lived. I offer it as such here:

> Under all circumstances we conduct ourselves as God's helpers, whether it be under much pressure or in hardships or great need or difficulties. God has shared this responsibility with us, [so] we are not going to chicken out now.
>
> Through it all we stand with sincerity, kindness, open-faced love, and the power of God. We are have-nots who have it all. We are paupers who enrich everybody. We are corpses with a lot of wiggle left. We are people who just won't die.[5]

Notes

1. Joyce Hollyday, "The Dream that Has Endured," *Sojourners* 8/12 (December 1979).

2. "A Brief History," http://www.koinoniapartners.org/History/brief.html (accessed 28 June 2010).

3. Millard Fuller, *Theology of the Hammer* (Macon GA: Smyth & Helwys, 1994) 7.

4. Millard Fuller, *Building Materials for Life*, vol. 3 (Macon GA: Smyth & Helwys, 2007) 7–8.

5. Clarence Jordan, *Cotton Patch Gospel: Paul's Epistles* (Macon GA: Smyth & Helwys, 2004) 77.

Part 1

Chattahoochee Valley Boy

(1956 and earlier)

Chapter 1

A Million Dollars

"Congratulations."

"For what?"

"You're a millionaire! Here's the financial statement. See for yourself."

Marilyn Black, secretary-treasurer of our company, was excitedly telling me that I had made it.

"We've just completed statements for the company and for you personally, and you're worth a million dollars! Isn't that wonderful?"

It was early fall in 1964. Hot outside, but not inside. We were cool. Sitting in a plush, cushioned chair on thick carpets, in an air-conditioned paneled office with a huge oak desk sprawled out in front of me, indeed, I thought it was wonderful!

A millionaire before the age of thirty. Co-owner of a prosperous, dynamic publishing and direct mail business in Montgomery, Alabama. No serious problems in business. Everything going my way. A financial statement showing my worth at a million dollars. Who wouldn't agree that such a state of affairs was wonderful? Every young man in the state of Alabama—in the whole nation, for that matter— would envy me if he knew.

Marilyn stood there for a moment, beaming. She was happy because I was happy. She was that way.

Miss Marilyn Black walked into my office for the first time in November 1962. Our business and law offices were then located near downtown Montgomery in an old house that we had converted into an office building. We had only ten employees. Marilyn had interviewed for the job of typist and receptionist.

When I first met Marilyn, she was not exuberant. She was quiet and correct in her manners. I remember that she was very young and had long black hair. I asked a lot of questions that first day. She answered everything with pleasant seriousness. Among other things, she gave the names of several references. After the interview, she left to return to her place of employment at the time.

I thought about the interview for a few minutes and decided to hire her without making any reference checks. I waited long enough for her to return to her office, then picked up the phone and dialed. I told her she was hired. That was that.

Marilyn Black started to work for Fuller & Dees Company and Dees and Fuller Attorneys-at-Law the next week.

My assessment of her was not wrong. If anything, I underestimated her ability. She tore through work. A fast typist, accurate, serious about her work, diligent, and efficient in every way, she quickly learned her way around the company, which was growing and fast becoming the most important phase of our activities.

When we had to replace our office manager in early 1963, Marilyn was offered the job. She cried that day in my office. She was afraid of the responsibility of supervising an office force that had by then grown to more than twenty people.

My business partner, Morris Dees, came in to help me plead with Marilyn to take the promotion. She finally accepted and immediately moved into her new job with renewed vigor. She cried some more in the weeks ahead, but she learned quickly and soon was doing a great job.

On this particular day, her appearance had not changed, but she had matured a lot, learned a lot, and climbed to the top in our young, rapidly expanding company. She was the youngest corporation officer in the city and one of the best. Marilyn was secretary-treasurer of our various corporations and dealt with all phases of her responsibilities as if she owned the entire operation. She had come a long way since her first visit to our office in 1962. So had the company. And so had I.

Marilyn was happy because I had a million-dollar financial statement, and I was happy about that, too.

Chapter 2

A Little More

"What's your next goal?" Marilyn asked.

"Ten million." I wrote it down in big numbers on a yellow pad.

Marilyn smiled, congratulated me again, and quickly walked out, easing the door closed behind her.

I was alone and ready to go to work on that next nine million. But I didn't start to work on it. I started thinking.

I thought deeply for a while. *What is happening in my life? Where am I going?* I wondered about ultimate values. *What is really important in life? Is it a million dollars, a big company, prestige, position in town, respect? Is it a financial statement showing a ten-million-dollar worth? What should I be doing with my life and with my time? Am I going after the right things in life by seeking a higher financial goal? Will I be satisfied with ten million, or will that lead me to seek yet a higher figure?*

Someone once asked John D. Rockefeller how much money is enough. He replied, "Just a little more."

I think I knew the answers to the questions swirling around in my head, but I wasn't about to admit to them honestly. I had it made, and it would be crazy—utter stupidity—to consider seriously another path in life.

I decided to go all out for that next nine million.

Perhaps it was at this moment that I crossed the invisible line separating the successful businessman from the man addicted to making money. Maybe it happened earlier; I don't know for sure. But I did begin to be at least vaguely aware, about this time, that money had become a god to me and that other values in my life fell in line somewhere behind it. I wasn't about to admit my deep thoughts to anyone, though, so I kept them inside, trying to hide them even from myself.

This was hard to do.

I remember that these same concerns, these same questions, had bothered me a few weeks earlier during the first week of August. The occasion that prompted my thinking that morning was a letter and a visit to my office by another young lady, my secretary Carol Burlingame.

For me, the most exciting time of the workday has always been opening the morning mail. There is a certain air of mystery and excitement about letters. "What great news will be borne by that little blue envelope, or the letter from Birmingham, or the manila envelope from Chicago?" That day it was a letter from Philadelphia, dated July 30, 1964. I tore open the envelope. It was from Jim Waery, secretary of the Speakers Bureau of the United Church of Christ.

I began to read.

He said I had been recommended by our church conference in the southeast United States to go overseas to visit missionaries. Upon my return, I would be expected to give of some of my time to traveling around and speaking to churches, church conferences, and other groups about what I had seen and experienced on the trip. I put the letter on my desk and let my mind explore the possibilities. I wanted to go, no doubt about it, and I knew where I wanted to go. Africa!

Africa!

I had been thinking for weeks and months about going to that great "dark continent," not to visit missionaries and see their work, but to shoot an elephant, a lion, a leopard, and lots more. I had started reading books on Africa and especially books about big game on the continent. The more I read, the less interested I became in making a trip to shoot big game because so much of the game there has been decimated. I knew I would feel guilty if I joined the crowd that was there to kill and destroy.

This letter from Philadelphia revived my interest in the trip. Now I had an opportunity to go and see. Visit missionaries. Talk to Africans. Maybe take pictures of elephants, lions, and leopards instead of killing them. And, upon my return, tell about all these experiences to groups across the country. This was something I could do well. It was something I wanted to do. It was a task that needed to be done because so many people knew little about church work beyond the city limits of their communities.

My name was suggested to the Speakers Bureau, I suppose, because of my involvement in the church, both in Montgomery and throughout the Southeast. My wife, Linda, and I had helped organize a United Church of Christ in our home early in 1961. I had been president of the Churchmen's Fellowship in the Southeast Conference since 1963. Before that, I was president of the Youth Organization in the Southeast Conference. (This conference comprises the churches of the United Church of Christ in Alabama, Georgia, South Carolina, Tennessee, Kentucky, and part of Florida.) I was a supporter of missionary work and had spoken many times throughout the conference on missions and other subjects.

All these thoughts raced through my head as I pondered the letter and the opportunities it opened for me. This was a chance to serve—perform a useful task for the church—while doing something I wanted to do anyway. This was something I could do well. I ought to go.

Then I had other thoughts. What would this trip cost? I was not too concerned about out-of-pocket expenses, such as plane tickets, meals, and lodging. My salary from the company was approaching a hundred thousand dollars a year. I could afford these things, even if the national office of the church didn't pay for them. But the company was in a tremendous burst of growth. Sales were increasing rapidly, as were profits. What would it cost me in terms of lost income to be away from the company for two or three months? I scribbled some figures on a note pad.

Another factor was my wife. Linda was enrolled at nearby Huntingdon College, completing requirements for a degree in elementary education. She wouldn't be able to go with me for that reason, plus the fact that we had two young children, a son Chris, age four, and a daughter Kim, age two.

We were beginning to have troubles in our marriage. Early in July, Linda had come to the office to tell me she didn't love me anymore.

At first I thought she was kidding, but when I realized she was serious, I was stunned and shocked beyond words. I agonized over this turn of events from that day forward. Clearly, I had many factors to consider before I agreed to go on the trip.

After thinking it over for a few more minutes, I picked up the phone and dialed Carol, my secretary. "Come in. I want to dictate a letter." I began when Carol was ready, "Dear Mr. Waery, Thank you for your letter of July 30. First, let me say that I am very appreciative of and humbled by the confidence that Dr. Lightbourne and Rev. Johnson have in me. I assure you and them that I am most grateful for the excellent opportunity you have placed before me. I would be delighted to visit some of our mission projects abroad. Unfortunately . . . ." Then I explained why I couldn't go. Naturally, I gave him only the business reasons.

The letter I wrote was almost two pages. Finally, I said I hoped he would keep the offer open, because I would possibly like to go in about two years when I felt it would be more convenient for me. I told Carol what stationery to use for the letter (we used about six different letterheads for various corporations) and dismissed her.

She hurried out and closed the door.

Chapter 3

Two Dreams

Leaning back in my chair, I started thinking again. Deep inside I felt a tinge of sadness. A tremendous opportunity had dropped in on me that morning; an opportunity for service was mine to give. In a real sense, a call from God had been made at my door, and I had turned him away. In many situations, is not a call simply a realization of a need and an agreement that you have the ability to fill that need if you are only willing to do so? Yes, I had received a call and had turned it down.

Now my mind drifted back to my college days at the University of Alabama and to an evening in my room when I had made a covenant with myself and with God. In that agreement, I solemnly promised that regardless of the success and money that came to me from a business that I was starting with Morris Dees, a fellow student—a business that seemed filled with promise of great success and much money—I would always seek the kingdom of God *first*. I covenanted that I would always share my money generously and would not become greedy and selfish as I had seen many other wealthy people become. I would not allow the business or success to interfere with my service to God.

I had made a covenant to put God first in my life, and now a real-life situation was confronting me. What was my priority? Business! I knew deep inside that this wasn't the first time.

When I was six years old, my father, an independent grocer just outside the little town of Lanett, Alabama (serving the community of Coleville and surrounding area), started me in business by buying me a pig and saying, "Son, you raise him, and you can make yourself some money."

I raised that pig. Every morning and every evening, I dutifully "slopped" that little pig until he became a hog. My father sold feed to me "on credit" from his store. He helped with record keeping and showed me how to "figure" and keep accurate cost records. When we estimated that the hog weighed the desired weight of two hundred pounds, we took him to market. I got my check and my father sat down with me to determine my profit. I had made just over eleven dollars (worth much more in 1941 than today)!

I continued in the hog-raising business until junior high school. Almost every hog I raised fetched more profit, and I dutifully put the money into a savings account.

In seventh grade, I took out most of my savings to invest in domesticated rabbits. Over a period of three years, I built up a rabbit population in our back yard of more than a hundred. I sold dressed rabbits around town to restaurants and in my father's store, and live baby rabbits to children for pets. I always did a booming business in selling young rabbits around Easter time

The rabbit business had its problems. At one time, many of my rabbits developed a severe case of ear sores. Huge scaly patches developed in both ears and the condition worsened until the ears finally drooped over. My rabbits looked awful. Can you imagine a pen of droopy-eared rabbits? Some began to die, and I was afraid this new disease would wipe me out. A county agent eventually gave me the answer—a 2 percent solution of salicylic acid applied to the sore areas of the ear once a day. The cure was complete and amazingly fast. Almost overnight, all the droopy ears perked up, and I had decent-looking rabbits again.

I was exuberant.

Another crisis developed when dogs started tearing into my pens and killing the rabbits. One night dogs ripped open a pen with young rabbits that were nearly ready to market and devoured fourteen of them. When I discovered this tragedy early the following morning, I rushed back in the house to tell Daddy. He was furious. I learned just how furious later that afternoon when I returned from school.

Our house was about a hundred yards down the hill from the store. I always got off the school bus in front of the store. The first thing I did every day was go in the store to get a soft drink or a piece of candy and learn the day's news.

"Where's Daddy?"

My stepmother, who frequently ran the store, said in an urgent tone, "He's at the house."

I didn't wait for an explanation. I could tell from the tone of her voice and the expression on her face that something was wrong.

Bursting through the house, I found my dad sitting on the back porch, solemn jawed, with a rifle across his lap. In front of him was a huge pile of dead dogs. "I've got fourteen dogs so far," he announced. He'd been sitting there all day with that rifle, shooting every dog that came by.

I dragged dead dogs out of the backyard until dark.

We didn't have any more trouble with dogs killing rabbits.

The next episode I experienced with my rabbits could have cost my life. Out behind the house was a spigot where I got water for them. Late one afternoon, in that period of twilight when it is neither light nor dark, I placed my watering bucket under the spigot, turned it on and stepped back to wait for it to fill up. Something hit my foot and I immediately felt a terrific stinging sensation. I jumped and looked back to see what had happened. It was a snake! I started screaming at the top of my voice, "Help! Help! A snake!" Almost instantly, our neighbor who lives down the hill from our house, emerged from his back door. With his face lathered and holding a straight razor, he raced up to me, grabbed my foot, and slashed it open. My stepmother had also heard my wails. She came running up with a pail of kerosene. They stuck my foot down in the kerosene to draw out the poison. It drew out the poison but it drew out a whole lot more blood. The ground around us looked like the ground at an old-fashioned hog killing!

In a few minutes, my dad wheeled up with his delivery truck. They tossed me in the front seat and off we raced to the hospital.

"I can't do anything," the doctor said. "You've done all that needs to be done. He'll be all right. I doubt if he'll even be sick." I never was. Scared but not sick. I learned that the snake was a young rattler. Prompt action had averted a possible tragedy.

During my early years of high school, I was able to fill fairly regular orders for rabbit meat from local restaurants. I became so skilled at dressing rabbits that I could have them skinned and gutted with some of the hearts still pumping as I raked remains in a pail.

I was in the tenth grade when Daddy bought a four-hundred-acre farm eight miles out of town. That's when I went out of the rabbit business. I wasn't too sorry, either, because I was getting tired of feeding twice a day and continuously cleaning stinking rabbit pills out of the pens. On rainy days, especially, I hated to go out to the pens. Nothing smells worse than rabbit pens on a rainy day.

With my savings and the money I realized from the sale of my final stock of rabbits—and the pens—I bought fifteen cows and turned them loose on the farm. Boy, what a great business that was! No more feeding, except a once-a-day provision of hay in the winter. No pens to clean out and the great outdoors to roam in while periodically checking on the cows.

My dad encouraged me all the way. I continued to keep books and turn a dollar into two and then into three. I developed a real love for business and for making money before graduating from high school. My dad and I talked a lot about making money and about business. He spent a lot of time with me. My mother had died suddenly when I was three years old, and my father tried to be mother and father to me after that. He remarried when I was six, but I was never able to develop a close relationship with my stepmother.

While I operated my own little business of raising pigs, rabbits, and cows, I helped my dad with his business. On Saturdays and weekdays after school, I worked in the store delivering orders of groceries on a bicycle and then, after I got a driver's license, in our delivery truck. I must admit that I was never enamored of the grocery business. In fact, I vowed in high school never to own or work in a grocery store.

Daddy did a great job of teaching me about business and of motivating me to be self-reliant and self-starting. He encouraged me to be thrifty and to save. "A dollar saved is a dollar made," he would always say. Waste of anything—time, a little hog feed, a needless trip, dogs killing rabbits—upset him more than anything.

A dollar was important to my father, and he worked for his. But he was generous and would open up his pocketbook for a person in need. He always gave generously to the church. He had a big heart, and he loved children as much as any man I've ever known. Hundreds of times, I saw him pick up a little child, hold him over a cookie jar he always kept on the front desk of the store, and let him grab out all he could hold. My dad's face was absolutely aglow as he watched the child walk out of the store with his two hands packed full of cookies.

Yes, I have a deep love for this man who had a great influence on my life. I am forever indebted to him for so many lessons and values he gave me as I grew up.

Chapter 4

Junior Achievement

Another influence on my business thinking was Junior Achievement. J.A., as it is called, is a youth business organization whose purpose is to teach teenagers about the American free enterprise system. Small groups of high school students form miniature companies and go into business for themselves. J.A. companies sell stock, produce a product, sell it, possibly make a profit, liquidate it at the end of each school year, and, in the process, learn what it means to be "in business."

I first learned about this program as a junior at Lanett (Alabama) High School. Two Junior Achievement staff men explained the program to an assembly of students. It sounded good to me. I already had some knowledge of business, but I wanted to know more. I signed up. The program was exciting to me, and I pitched myself wholeheartedly into it. Starting in September, several members of our J.A. formed a "company." We met once a week until May. We manufactured campstools and watering cans. We made the latter by scraping and painting beer cans and welding copper tubing into the cans for a spout and handle. I became president of the company.

At the end of the first year in the program, I was selected as one of four delegates from our area to attend the National Conference of Junior Achievement held at Valley Forge, Pennsylvania. At this gathering, I met for the first time some of the big-name industrialists in America. Men such as Bayard Colgate and Edwin Mosler were walking around the place and talking to delegates about stocks, profits, production, and sales. I met bright kids from all over the United States, and everyone was interested in business. It was stimulating and exciting. I returned home after that conference "fired up" beyond words about Junior Achievement.

During my second year in J.A., my senior year in high school, I became involved in many extracurricular aspects of the program.

Webber Hudson, executive director of the local business center, used me that fall as his chief aide in recruiting young people for the program. I spoke to student assemblies in all three local high schools. Throughout the year, I spoke frequently at civic clubs on behalf of J.A. In the spring, Mr. Hudson asked me to give the report on our area at the regional conference in Atlanta. At the end of the year, he was instrumental in getting a partial scholarship for me to attend college. Later, when I was a student at Auburn University, Mr. Hudson hired me as program director of a new Junior Achievement program in Opelika, Alabama. At nineteen, I was the youngest director of such a program in the country.

In 1963, Mr. Hudson invited me to speak at his "Future Unlimited" Celebration in the War Memorial Auditorium in Nashville, Tennessee, where he was executive director of the J.A. program. When my business with partner Morris Dees was first starting at the University of Alabama, he was its number-one customer. He ordered all the merchandise he possibly could and encouraged others to do likewise. He wrote letters to people all over the country on behalf of our new company, urging them to buy our products.

In 1964, when I was the keynote speaker at the 21st National Junior Achievement Conference at Indiana University, Webber Hudson introduced me. In these and many other ways, Mr. Hudson opened doors of opportunity for me. He and I became good friends, and I am grateful to him for the interest he took in me and for the encouragement he gave me, both while I was in Junior Achievement and for years afterward.

By the end of my senior year in high school, as a result of pigs, rabbits, cattle, and Junior Achievement, I had developed a strong desire to go into business. I didn't know yet what kind of business, but I wanted it to be big, profitable, and successful. I wanted to be a millionaire, too. This would be the sure sign of success in business . . . and in life, as far as I was concerned.

Chapter 5

Church

At the same time I was engaging in my multifarious business pursuits, I was also attending church. Sunday and church went together in our family like ham and eggs or bread and butter. When Sunday came, we put on our "Sunday clothes" and went to Sunday school and church. Each Sunday night, we went back to the evening worship service. As a child, I don't ever remember thinking about *not* going to church on Sunday.

Our church was the Lanett Congregational Christian Church. It was situated in the middle of the little cotton mill town of Lanett, Alabama, which is located in east central Alabama, bordering Georgia. We lived on the edge of town and drove about two miles to church every Sunday. My mother had attended the church before she married. Her parents had been members of the church for years. My father had been a Baptist, but he changed over when he and Mother married.

I suppose the church was a rather ordinary one in the community. By and large, it reflected the culture of the area, and its people valued the things other local people valued and shared their prejudices. Some of the church people were warm and friendly. Others were grouchy. Most didn't care much about the overall work of the church. They came on most Sundays, and that was about it. One or two families rarely came to church. People talked about them and said how worried they were about them. All the talking did little good, though, because the families kept staying at home on Sundays—or going fishing. A few people worked hard for the church. They worried about its finances. They planned for growth and a new building. They fretted over apathy among other members and begged people to teach Sunday school and sing in the choir. Almost continuously there was a squabble going on among choir members about something or other. (I learned in later years that this description fits most churches.)

I remember most of my Sunday school classes as extreme exercises in futility. Many a Sunday, the teacher would come in the class and proceed to read the lesson in a monotone voice. Most of us in the class would tune her out within two minutes and become engaged in our own private pursuits, such as looking at each other and giggling, throwing spitballs across the room, and scribbling in our Sunday school books. When things got too out of hand, the teacher would make us take turns reading the lesson so she could watch us. What I enjoyed most was the fifteen-minute break between Sunday school and church.

Church was more fun than Sunday school. When I was very young, after my mother died and before my dad remarried, I used to stand in the choir with my dad. I felt bigger than all the other children in the church. I was special because I got to be in the choir. Daddy sang with the choir for a while, but then he didn't sing anymore. I think there was a big fuss about something. My daddy didn't like fusses, so he quit singing with them. After that, we sat together out in the congregation.

The seats were harder out there. I had a tough time sitting still. "Be still. Be still," my father said to me a thousand times. On two or three occasions, he took me down to the basement to "wear me out." Finally, I really made him angry. He ran down the stairs with me and beat me so badly that I never forgot it. I was quiet as a mouse in church from that day on.

As I grew older, I became bored with the church service. I couldn't stay awake. I fell asleep almost every Sunday. One morning my head bobbed lower and lower and lower. Just before it touched the pew in front of me, I awakened suddenly. My body jerked backward with such suddenness that my head popped forward like the end of a whip. "Crack!" My head crashed into the pew with such a force that it startled the preacher. I'm sure I woke up everyone else in the church. In any event, I was kidded about my noisy sleep for several months.

My sleeping in church got me in trouble on another occasion. Every summer the church held a revival. We'd go every night for a week to hear a visiting revivalist preach a sermon. One year, an old minister, Reverend Gray, was our preacher. I liked him, but some of his sermons put me to sleep like the regular sermons did. One night he started in preaching and I promptly went to sleep. I awakened when the choir started singing at the end of the service. My friend, Rev. Gray, was down in the front of the pulpit smiling and asking for people to come forward and shake his hand. No one came. I thought this was terrible. This man was pleading for people to come up and shake his hand and no one would go. I stepped out of my place and walked up to him and shook his hand. He seemed pleased.

After the closing prayer was given, people started coming up to me and telling me how proud they were for what I'd done. I was puzzled. I didn't think it was so great to shake hands with Rev. Gray. I had shaken his hand before and no one had congratulated me.

That night at home my father sat me down, and in a grave, urgent tone, he began asking me if I knew what it meant to be a church member. I said, "No, why?"

"You joined the church tonight!"

While I was still asleep, Rev. Gray had issued a call for people to come forward and give their lives to Christ.

"But Daddy," I exclaimed, "I went forward only to shake his hand!"

After we talked a little longer, my father suggested I wait a few years before joining the church. I agreed.

A few years later, at age thirteen, I joined the church and was baptized by immersion.

I should explain that it is the general practice in Congregational churches to baptize infants and "confirm" them at ages twelve to sixteen. In most southern Congregational churches, however, the practice does not include baptizing infants. Only adults and youths who are "old enough" to understand their choice are baptized, and frequently by immersion. In other parts of the country, baptism by immersion in Congregational churches (later called United Church of Christ) is practically unknown.

One summer a little redheaded preacher from North Carolina came to our church to conduct a revival. I didn't sleep during his sermons. He was a one-man show. After a few opening hymns, he'd jump up, talk long enough to work up a good sweat, take off his coat, burst into a song, talk some more, sing some more, and so on until the end of the service. He was great! I had heard lots of talk about Jesus in Sunday school and from the pulpit, but this man talked like he knew Jesus. He talked about Jesus in such a personal way that I thought for sure he had actually seen him and lived when he did. It was only much later, long after the revival, that I realized that he did not, in fact, know Jesus as a natural living person. He knew him all right, but not the way I thought. Jesus made a difference in that man's life, and it was plain for all to see. I'll never forget the joy I saw in that man's face when he talked about Jesus, his friend.

With all its frailties, through men like the redheaded preacher and the Sunday school teacher with a monotone voice, church was a definite influence on my life, even in my early years. Seeds were planted there that matured through the years, and I am grateful for them. I hear many people lambasting the "institutional" church. I heartily agree with many of the deficiencies that are pointed out. The church is vulnerable. It needs criticism. The Lanett Congregational Christian Church was—and still is—vulnerable and in need of renewal. But, more important, the church needs committed people who will work with diligence to reform and renew it.

The question facing the Lanett church and the church universal is not whether it is going out of existence. Rather, it is whether the church is going to fulfill its divine task with both faith and courage and whether it is going to perform the task half-heartedly through half-committed, timid, apathetic, apologetic people. The question simply is whether or not the church is going to do a good job or a poor job of proclaiming God's word to our age, and especially to our youth.

My active participation in the church and Sunday school continued through junior high and senior high school. But, except for an occasional church summer camp and infrequent visits to other churches in our area, my experiences were limited to our church in Lanett.

Chapter 6

Beyond Lanett

In 1953, while a senior in high school, I was asked to attend the annual meeting of the Southeast Conference of Congregational Christian Churches in Chattanooga, Tennessee, to lead a group of young people. The horizon of my church life was about to widen. At that little meeting of about thirty young people of high school and college age, we decided to form a youth organization separate from the adult conference. Prior to that time, the youth had no formal organization within the conference. No regular meetings or rallies were held for them. The only time any young people got together was when a few came to the annual conference with their parents.

I was "railroaded" in as president of our new "organization." We decided to call it the "Pilgrim Fellowship of the Southeast Conference."

After the weekend conference was over, we returned to our homes and resumed life as usual. I kept waiting for someone to tell me what to do as president. I waited all year. No one told me anything, so I did nothing. Next spring, the conference met again, this time at my home church in Lanett. The young people—many of whom were present the year before in Chattanooga—traveled to Georgia to the Pine Mountain Boy Scout Camp for our sessions. We talked more about our "organization." I reported that I hadn't done anything during the year because I didn't know what to do. I had received no guidance from anyone. After hearing my sad report, they elected me president again! I objected, but they insisted, saying, "There is no one else to do the job."

After this weekend, conference ended, and we returned to our homes again, but this time I was determined to do something about our youth organization. I didn't wait for anyone to give me approval to act or suggest what I should do. I wrote letters, went to see people, and mapped out plans for a conference-wide youth rally in the Lanett church. This conference was held a year later in March 1955. One hundred seventy young people came! We had a great program with speakers from all over the country. I was overjoyed. I didn't object when they elected me president again because I wanted to build up the organization and make it permanent.

I entered Auburn University in the fall of 1953. During that year, sandwiched between college studies at Auburn University, a job as program director of Junior Achievement in nearby Opelika, Alabama, and a hundred other things, I plowed ahead with work on our Pilgrim Fellowship organization. I nailed a map of the southeast United States on the wall of my college room and pinpointed our churches. I compiled a list of key young people and group leaders. I started sending periodic newsletters to all of them. I drew lines on my map, outlining five districts within the conference. Then I went to work setting up a series of youth rallies in each of these districts to be held each quarter. There were dozens of meetings to attend and a lot of traveling to do. Practically every weekend I was off to some part of the conference to attend a meeting or speak before a group. Then there was the second big annual Pilgrim Fellowship Conference to be held in spring 1956. We had decided to hold it back in Chattanooga, where we had started the idea three years earlier. Almost two hundred and fifty young people came! It was a celebration for those of us who had started in the small group in 1953. I was pleased to hand over the gavel to the new president, V. R. Dobson, at the end of this confer-ence. I felt that our organization was sound and strong and that it would continue.

It has continued to be a significant influence in the lives of a great many young people in the churches of the Southeast. In 1965, I was privileged to speak at the closing banquet of the tenth annual Pilgrim Fellowship Conference in Birmingham, Alabama. That was a great thrill for me.

My three-year term as president of the Pilgrim Fellowship was a tremendous experience and a deep spiritually enriching period in my life. I met and worked with some of the finest people I have ever known. Erston Butterfield, the conference minister, was a terrific man and a great Christian. He wouldn't tell me what to do, but he was always willing to listen to a problem or suggest a better way to do something. During the first half of my term as president, there was no staff person in the conference to work with the young people. In 1955, Reverend Annie Campbell joined the staff as Christian education director. She was an enormous help to us in too many ways to mention, but, even better, she was a practicing, joyful, ever optimistic, dynamic Christian. I'll never forget and will always love Annie Campbell. There are countless young people in the South who feel the same way.

Most important are the young people who worked so diligently to bring about an active youth group in our conference. Mary Stewart of Pleasant Hill, Tennessee, was vice president one year. Betty Slater of Chattanooga, Tennessee, was treasurer. Bill Green of Roanoke, Alabama, wrote hundreds of letters as secretary. V. R. Dobson of Lanett was vice president in 1955 and assumed the presidency in 1956. All of these people and many more worked with great energy and devotion to make the Pilgrim Fellowship a living force in the conference.

As president, I traveled constantly. I spent many nights in the homes of total strangers all through the South, but these people accepted me as a son. I was working for the church, and they were glad to give me a place to spend the night. I learned the meaning of Christian fellowship through firsthand experience.

I did a great deal of traveling by hitchhiking. We didn't have much money in our treasury—certainly not enough for extensive travel by the president—so I went by "air": "Aire you going my way?" I had some interesting and often hair-raising experiences on the road. That I survived all my travels is good evidence that God was traveling with me!

Chapter 7

Hitchhiking

One time, I was traveling from Chattanooga to Lanett. Just south of Chattanooga, a man in a black Cadillac stopped for me. I jumped in and off we roared. In just a few moments we were traveling at a terrific speed. He was talking his head off and looking at me more than at the road. I quickly realized that he had been drinking. When I was able to get in a word, I suggested that he stop the car and let me drive. "All right," he said, slamming on the brakes. "You drive, but go at least eighty. If you don't I'll take over the driving again." I slid under the wheel and off we raced. Highway 27 just south of Chattanooga is laden with deep curves. Driving eighty miles an hour is a thrill to say the least, but I didn't want him to drive at that speed and I didn't want to give up the ride. I slowed for some of the curves. "I said go eighty!" he'd shout. All the while, he was drinking one can of beer right after another. He had almost a full case in the back seat of the car. Every few miles he'd yell, "Stop the car!" I'd slam on the brakes; he'd stumble out into the bushes, urinate, crawl back in, and mutter, "Let's go."

He said he was Herbert Hoover's nephew and that he was going to see his sick wife in Florida. When we got to Rome, Georgia, he directed me to a remote section of town. We pulled up to a house he pointed out. "This is a whorehouse," he announced. "You want to come in with me? It'll be good for you." I said I didn't care to and that I thought he shouldn't go in. He wanted to know why. We had a long discussion on the subject, but he decided to go in anyway. I waited in the car. After a while he came back out, laughing loudly. He told me he had told the "ladies" that he had an innocent young Christian in the car and they wanted me to come in. They would provide services for me free of charge. I declined. He pulled on my arm, insisting that

I go. After a long argument, he gave up and staggered back in to tell them I wouldn't come in. In a few minutes he returned and we continued our fast ride south.

As we approached LaGrange, Georgia, I looked for a police car because I knew I would have to leave him there. I was going to go west to Lanett, and he would be continuing south toward Florida. I had pleaded with him to let me leave him at a motel to sleep off his drunk. He wouldn't hear of it. I wanted to have him arrested for his own safety. Unfortunately, I could not find a single police car. I got out in the middle of LaGrange. He slid under the wheel and raced off so fast that his tires squealed. I said a prayer for him and could only hope he made it to his destination.

In 1954, Albert Van Cleave of Wadley, Alabama, was chosen along with me to attend the National Youth Conference at Yale University in Connecticut. We decided to hitchhike. I had the wildest ride of my life on this trip. We were in North Carolina, and a sleek convertible pulled over for us. We jumped in. The driver was a pretty young girl, about eighteen years old. She pushed the accelerator to the floorboard, and off we raced. Traffic was heavy. She got up to about seventy miles an hour, weaving dangerously in and out of traffic. Albert and I began to look worriedly at each other.

"Why are you going so fast and driving so reckless?" I inquired.

"Well," she announced, "my mother just told me she isn't going to buy me a new car this year, so I'm going to wreck this one. Then she'll have to buy me a new one.

"Not with us in here," I said. "Stop this car and let us out."

"No."

"Stop!" I demanded.

She angrily stomped on the brakes and came to a screeching halt. We jumped out and on she raced, determined to wreck her car so she could get a new one!

In summer 1956, I did a great deal more hitchhiking. At the encouragement of Rev. Campbell, I took a job as "student summer service worker" with our National Board of Home Missions. That summer was the busiest, most rewarding, and most exhilarating one of my life. Practically every day was packed with adventure and excitement.

From June until September, I traveled from Lanett to Pomona and Pleasant Hill, Tennessee; to Crete, Nebraska; to Wadley, Caddo, Steele, and Thorsby, Alabama; to Gaillard, Georgia; to Chicago, Illinois; and to Salisbury, North Carolina, before returning home. Along the way, I counseled at a summer camp, attended two national youth conferences, taught a course on parliamentary procedure at a youth camp, conducted five Bible schools, led singing at a revival, preached several times, attended the Democratic National Convention, recovered a drowned boy from a lake, attended two funerals, hitchhiked thousands of miles, spent the night in a broken-down school bus on a lonely road in West Virginia, and started and completed a college correspondence course in political science.

My summer work started the first week in June at Camp Pomona, Tennessee, in the Cumberland Mountains near Crossville. There, I had been a counselor to a group of "toad-frog" boys. I call them "toad-frog" boys because they were at the age of jumping around constantly. One little boy in my group learned that he could bounce higher and higher on his bed until he reached the rafters in our barracks. Once in the attic, he would race around knocking dust and other debris out onto all the beds in the room. After tiring of this "fun," he would leap onto another boy's bed, usually breaking it down. We lost several beds this way before I caught the culprit.

Between episodes with my boys, I attended a course on Bible school teaching techniques.

From Camp Pomona I went to nearby Pleasant Hill, Tennessee, where I conducted a two-week Bible school at the community church. Since it was my first Bible school, I had an unusually busy time of making everything run smoothly.

Pleasant Hill is an interesting little mountain community. It is church centered, with many activities, both religious and secular, held in the church building. The community owned a farm, a craft shop, and a guesthouse. Quite a number of retired people had homes in the area. The whole community seemed concerned for the welfare of these seniors among them. A genuine neighborliness existed in Pleasant

Hill. Dr. Mae Wharton, author of *Woman Doctor of the Cumberlands*, lived and practiced medicine there. All the people were lovely. I've never met warmer, friendlier people than the great folks at Pleasant Hill. The pastor of the church was Paul Reynolds. He and his wife had been missionaries to China for fifteen years before coming to Pleasant Hill after the Communist takeover in China. Paul Reynolds and his wife were truly saintly people. They were Christians in the full sense of the word and lived it out every day of their lives. One night they had me over to their home for dinner. We sat cross-legged on the floor and, with chopsticks, ate the best Chinese meal I've ever tasted.

Most of the time I stayed in the guesthouse. The Davises were hosts in the house at that time. We had many great times together telling stories, exchanging experiences, gazing out over the green mountainside, and enjoying the cool mountain breezes. I'll never forget one story Mrs. Davis told about her father. It seems that he had never been to church. Even though they lived in the house nearest the church, he would not attend. Then the church had a terrible fuss about something, and half the members pulled out to form another church. This dissident group acquired land on the other side of her father's house and started building. Late one afternoon, some of the deacons of the new church were walking home after a day of working on the church building. They met Mrs. Davis's father coming from the other direction.

"Well," the men said to him, "I guess we'll get you in church now that we have a church on both sides of your house."

"Yes," he replied, "I suppose so. It was a group about like you that cornered Christ and nailed him to a tree."

After Pleasant Hill, I went to Nashville where I met Rev. E. Campbell and three young people. The five of us drove from there to Doane College in Crete, Nebraska, for the National Pilgrim Fellowship Conference. Our arrival at the conference was marked by an incident I'll never forget. As we drove into the parking space near the registration area, Jean McCarter spotted us. Jean was a beautiful Negro girl from Southern California who had been elected national vice resident at the Yale Conference two years earlier. I had met her there. She rushed over to the car and greeted all of us warmly. After several minutes of introduction and small talk, she said, "Follow me. I'll take you to registration." She turned and started walking away, and I followed. One of the young men with us, V. R. Dobson, tapped me on the shoulder and beckoned with his finger that he wanted to say something. I stopped. Cupping his hand around my ear, he put his mouth up close and whispered, "Hey, I've never seen a nigger like that before!"

I've thought about this episode many times since then. The impact with this experience on V. R. Dobson is precisely the impact that contact with people like Jean McCarter had on me. I attribute my present attitudes on race largely to my many interracial contacts in regional and national Pilgrim Fellowship conferences. Seeds of ideas about the worth of people regardless of race were planted firmly in my mind at these conferences. Some of these seeds did not germinate until much later, but I have no doubt about the time of their planting.

I was nominated at this conference for national president. I felt greatly honored and flattered, but I asked to be excused from the election because I would be a senior in college the following year. The term lasted for two years, and I didn't know at the time what I would do the year after graduation. Anyway, I felt that a younger person ought to be president. I was getting "old."

The conference was going great. Then, on Wednesday, I got an urgent phone call from home advising that my father's only brother had died suddenly of a heart attack. Someone drove me to the airport in Omaha.

My last Pilgrim Fellowship Conference as a "youth" came to an abrupt end.

After my uncle's funeral, I went to Southern Union College in nearby Wadley, Alabama, to teach a course in parliamentary procedure at a weeklong church camp for high school boys and girls. Then I hitchhiked to Caddo in North Alabama.

The minister of the small First Congregational Christian Church in Caddo was E. T. Shelton. I stayed in his home during the week while conducting a Bible school in his church.

Rev. and Mrs. Shelton had ten children ranging in age from two to twenty-one years old. All ten still lived at home. I joined the fun. Everybody couldn't fit in the kitchen at one time, so we ate in shifts. Two of the younger children gave up their double bed for me and slept on the floor. Each child had specific chores. It was a hectic but happy family. (Needless to say, Rev. Shelton had another job in addition to being pastor of the church!) Mrs. Shelton was one of the happiest women I have ever met. She smiled, sang, or hummed all the time and was as trim as could be. In spite of all the work she had at home, she took one of the assignments at the church as a Bible school teacher and did a wonderful job.

I left Caddo smiling, for it was a happy week and a good experience.

I had indeed been busy so far that summer, but my most exciting week was yet to come.

Chapter 8

Raising the Dead

The most exciting week was the one I spent at Mount Lebanon Congregational Church near Steele, Alabama. I went to this little church on top of Chandler Mountain, a few miles north of Birmingham, to conduct a Bible school. We had our Bible school all right, and it was a good one, but that just begins to tell the story at Mount Lebanon.

A revival was under way. The minister, Rev. Elmer Smith, was conducting it and preaching most of the sermons. He was a small man in stature, but a powerful man in voice and spirit. On a typical night, the service would start with the singing of several familiar hymns. I was the song leader. After every couple of hymns, someone would be called upon to say a prayer. At the conclusion of this period of hymn singing and prayers, we would enter into a time of testifying. Rev. Smith would issue an invitation to people in the congregation to tell what the Lord had done for them. Every night the same people got up and told the same stories. Sometimes a new person would say a word or two, but you could always count on certain ones.

After the "testifying" was over, we'd have a sermon. Sometimes Rev. Smith would preach. At other times, he would invite a visiting minister to preach. To the right of the pulpit was a long pew. Visiting preachers of other denominations sat there and said "Amen" at strategic points during the worship service. When Rev. Smith wanted one of these men to preach, he selected him on the spot and asked him to deliver the sermon. The man would come forward and, without any preparation, "hold forth" for an hour or more.

When Rev. Smith preached, it was a thriller. He had black beady eyes that could look right through a person. He would start off softly then build up to a shout again, maybe this time sustaining his thunderous roars for several minutes before breaking off to a normal level of speaking. From time to time, he'd grab the Bible and bang it across his open palm while explaining its message to the hushed congregation. Then he'd bend down low and shake it menacingly toward someone in the back row. Quickly he'd rush to the other side of the pulpit and shake it at people in another direction. When he wanted support, he would make a profound statement and look at the pew of visiting preachers. In unison, they would all loudly proclaim, "Amen!" Rev. Smith was quite a preacher, and he could move a congregation from tears to laughter to tears again within a snap of your fingers.

Following his sermon, Rev. Smith would issue a "call" to come forward and be "saved" or rededicate one's life to Christ. He would start in front of the pulpit and remind folks that Jesus was waiting on them and that tomorrow might be too late. His pleas were urgently issued over soft background singing of hymns such as "Softly and Tenderly Jesus Is Calling" or "Why Not Tonight." If someone came forward, there were shouts of "Praise God!" "Hallelujah!" "Thank the Lord!" Rev. Smith would ask that we continue to sing because "the Spirit was at work." Frequently, we would sing all verses of the same song four or five times.

After Rev. Smith was positively certain that no one else was coming forward, he would hold up his hands and call for quiet.

"This beloved brother (or sister) has come forward to give his life to Christ," he would announce solemnly. "He wishes to unite with this church and lead a Christian life. What is your wish? Do I hear a move that we accept him?"

"I so move."

"I second."

"All in favor say 'Aye.'"

"Aye."

"Welcome, brother."

Then, while the pianist played softly, everyone would file past the new convert to shake his hand. Relatives always made an emotional scene of hugging, crying, kissing, and carrying on like the person had died instead of being saved.

After everyone was thoroughly exhausted, physically, emotionally, and spiritually, Rev. Smith would call on someone—usually a visiting preacher—to say the closing prayer, after which we would all file out the double front door into the warm night air. People quickly dispersed as everyone was too tired to visit, and the sanctuary became as quiet as death.

Soon after the revival started, death did come to the community and to the church. We had just completed Bible school about noon one day when a group of us standing outside the church saw a cloud of dust billowing up in the distance along the unpaved road that ran in front of the church. Soon, an old car appeared in the distance traveling at a high speed. As we watched, it raced on toward the church and flew past.

"Where is that fool going?" we wondered. Just then, we heard him slam on brakes and slide to a fast halt. We could hear the car racing in reverse.

A young man was driving and one look into his face told us something was wrong.

"There is a boy drowning in the lake!"

"Where?"

"Down there"—he pointed—"in the lake."

"Let's go!"

I jumped in with a couple of other fellows. He turned around in the churchyard, and back down the road we raced.

"What happened?" we inquired.

The young man was choked up, and it was hard for him to talk. But he finally got out that he had been swimming in this lake with his buddy when, all of a sudden, his friend went down. He dove a couple of times for him and hadn't been able to locate him. So he swam to shore and came for help.

We slid to a halt at the lake's edge, jumped out, and asked where he went down.

"Over there."

A boat was on the shore. Three or four of us quickly stripped to our underclothes, jumped in the boat, and paddled to the spot he had indicated. We started diving. After two or three dives, the young man decided maybe his friend had gone down at a different place. We paddled there and dived. No luck. We knew we were racing against time, and everyone was desperate. A full half-hour later, we were still diving without success.

Our lungs felt as though they were bursting. "Let's try over here!"

Down went one of the young men. He came up and exclaimed, "I found him!"

"Where?"

"Right over there, but I can't bring him up."

He started crying. I jumped in the direction he pointed. Down, down. I touched his foot. I'll never forget that feeling. Groping along on the bottom of the lake feeling for a fellow human being—the feeling is indescribable. And then touching him! I grabbed him by his ankle and struggled. Coming up right beside the boat, I grabbed on with one hand and pulled the foot up out of the water with the other.

By this time, a large crowd had gathered on shore. When they saw that foot—a deep sickly purple—emerge from the water, a scream went up from the women that sent chills up my spine and made my hair stand on end. I was shaking like a leaf when I crawled into the boat.

Once on shore, we pulled him onto the ground and started administering artificial respiration. We kept it up for more than an hour, but it was no use. He was dead.

We learned later that the two young men had been at the lake drinking whiskey. They decided to take a swim. About halfway across the lake there was a ledge. A bulldozer had dug a deep hole on one side of the lake, leaving a ledge that dropped straight down to a depth of twelve to fifteen feet. Beyond the ledge, the water was only about two feet deep. Less than a yard from the ledge, the drowned young man had gone down. His friend reached the ledge, saw that his friend had gone down, made a couple of dives for him without success, and then swam to shore and drove for help.

The drowning had an electrifying effect on the revival. The young man was the son of a family in the church, and the funeral would be held there.

When the preacher talked about tomorrow being too late, people listened with renewed interest. There were urgent prayers for the family of the deceased and for the young man's soul. The testimonies in the services were longer and more fervent. Singing seemed louder. Preaching was stronger. More people joined the church, and many came forward to be "rededicated."

Chapter 9

Beyond Revival

The day of the funeral, cars came from far and wide. The churchyard was filled, with cars parked down the little dusty road in both directions. Not all the people could get inside that day. Many stood on the front steps and looked in. Others, mostly men smoking Camel cigarettes, stood around outside with one leg propped up on a car fender, talking in a low tones about cattle, crops, and the weather. I couldn't get in, so I talked with the men. Inside, you could hear the service progressing. First the singing, then praying, then the sermon. Finally the viewing of the body. Everyone filed by slowly, and from time to time you would hear a loud wail, "Lord, Lord, no. No. Oh, Lord! Lord have mercy." Then there was a final hymn, and the people followed the casket to the graveyard for a brief service there.

On the last night of the revival, a dramatic thing happened. At the conclusion of the preaching, Rev. Smith came down in front of the pulpit to issue his call for people to come forward and join the church. I was sitting on one of the front pews of the church and noticed a stirring among the people of the congregation. I turned around. There, shuffling slowly up the center aisle was an older woman, at least in her seventies. She was coming forward to join the church. When she reached Rev. Smith, she dropped to her knees and grabbed his hands. A younger woman rushed to her side and kneeled with her. The old woman was sobbing softly. The younger woman was crying loudly. At the end of the verse, Rev. Smith called for silence. He leaned over and spoke in hushed tones with the older woman for a long time. All you could hear in the church were soft sobs and the "swish, swish" of the hand fans the people used to try to keep cool.

After a long while, Rev. Smith rose slowly. "This good sister," he said, "is over seventy years old. She has never been a member of the church. She wants to unite with this church and give the remainder of her life to Christ. Her daughter has come to kneel with her in this important decision."

After the service, everyone was talking excitedly about how happy they were that this woman was finally coming into the church. She had been in the community all her life but had never become a Christian.

That was the best night of the revival.

The baptism of this woman was more dramatic than her joining the church. Late on Sunday afternoon of the last day of the revival, the people of the church met on the edge of a lake at the foot of Chandler Mountain to baptize those who had joined during the week. (This was not the lake where the drowning occurred.) We sang a few hymns, and Rev. Smith offered a brief sermon. Then he waded into the lake until the water was up to his waist. One by one, the converts waded out to be baptized.

The last person to go out was the old woman.

By the time it was her turn, evening shadows from the mountains were beginning to creep across the still waters. The sun was sinking low, and dim rays of sunlight streamed across the lake. It was a beautiful sight as the old woman carefully felt her way out to the preacher. I watched her face as she went. It was solemn and serious.

Rev. Smith reached out and grabbed her hand, pulling her close to his side. He placed one of her hands over her nose. Then he placed one of his hands behind her head and the other around her waist.

"I baptize you in the name of the Father, the Son, and the Holy Ghost."

Down she went. When she came up, dripping wet from head to toe, a broad smile filled every crevice of her timeworn face. Her arms went up and she burst forth to the top of her voice.

"Hallelujah! Hallelujah! Hallelujah! Hallelujah! Hallelujah!"

The hills echoed her cry of joy as her hallelujahs bounced from one to the next along the mountain. Whatever her past sins, they were gone—washed away—and she was overjoyed. She fairly ran out of the lake, smiling and swinging her arms erratically to maintain her balance as she sloshed through the water. Her daughter waited at the water's edge. They embraced warmly, crying and laughing all the while. Everyone looked on without moving or saying a word.

I bit my lip and choked back tears. This was the most moving religious experience in my life up to that time. I will never forget it.

On Monday morning as I waved good-bye to my new friends at Mt. Lebanon and stuck out my thumb for a ride south to Thorsby, Alabama, I wondered if the remainder of the summer would match my experiences so far.

That, I thought, would be hard to do.

Chapter 10

Separation

My exciting week at Mt. Lebanon was now history, and I was off to Thorsby, Alabama. Nothing spectacular happened in that small central Alabama town. We had a Bible school that ran for a week without fanfare or incident, and that was about it.

But at my next stop in Gaillard, Georgia, we had a "riot."

I arrived at this tiny South Georgia town on Sunday afternoon to start a Bible school on Monday at Pleasant Hill Congregational Church, a small rural church with about seventy-five members. After checking in at the home of my hosts for the week, I dashed off to the Sunday evening worship service. It was a "normal" service in every way except for the announcements. When that moment came in the order of worship, the minister said he had an important matter to put before the congregation. He pulled a letter out of his pocket. It was from Erston Butterfield, the conference minister. He began to read. The letter stated, first of all, that it was a private communication between the conference minister and the pastors of the conference regarding an important subject. The letter went on to ask for a private, personal opinion of the ministers regarding the acceptance of Negro churches into membership in the conference.

Mr. Butterfield made it clear that he was conducting a poll of ministers, not local members, but this pastor put the matter before the entire church! Upon completion of the reading, the preacher called for discussion. Speaker after speaker rose to declare they wanted no Negroes in their church. It was obvious to me that the question raised in the letter had never been discussed openly among the members of this congregation. Finally someone rose to propose a vote: "I move we never *segregate* this church."

"I second that."

"All those in favor say 'Aye.'"

"Aye."

Not a dissenting vote. No segregation in that church. They didn't understand the terms they were using, but they knew what they meant, if not what they said.

I confronted their meaning and resolve in this matter on two occasions during the week. A couple of the boys in the Bible school had Negro boys as playmates. They always came to Bible school together in the morning. Usually, they arrived early and played together in the churchyard before Bible school began. Then the little Bible school boys would come inside, leaving their friends outside to wait for them until they got out a couple of hours later. I didn't know what these Negro boys did during the two hours until about the middle of the week.

One day I asked one of my teachers, "Why do they go under the church and listen to our sessions through the floor?"

My ideas of racial justice were not firm at this time, but I felt something was wrong with this arrangement. I went to the deacons and requested that the boys be allowed to come in. The answer was a firm "No." They expressed no concern for the boys whatsoever. Under the house was where they belonged. "Oh, we don't have any objection to them hearing the lessons through the floor. Yes, let them sit under the church!"

Almost daily, after Bible school was over, the boys went swimming together in a nearby lake. They were fast friends all day, but they couldn't go to Bible school together in a Christian church.

Someone had given me a Brownie camera, so I took several pictures of this happy little integrated group and sent them to the conference office. On the back of the pictures I wrote, "We are having a race riot in Gaillard, Georgia." An accompanying letter explained the "riot." If this matter were not so tragic in its implications, it would be hilarious—a funny "riot." In a real sense, it was a "riot" in the more serious meaning of that term. There was more to come.

One night, I was a guest for dinner in the home of one of the leaders in the church. We began discussing race relations. I said only about two sentences, and my host became furious. He demanded to know who had sent me "down there" and where I was from. He said he thought I ought to leave his home and leave the church. When I told him I was born and raised in Alabama, he was bewildered. He couldn't understand what I was talking about or how I possibly could feel the way I did about Negroes. I was allowed to stay for the meal, but I am positive I would have been asked to leave if I had not used all the diplomacy at my command. It was a sticky evening, and for more reasons than the heat and humidity of summer!

Our Bible school continued to run smoothly, and we ended the week without further incident, but there was a pronounced coolness toward me by week's end. I was kind of glad to leave that little town on Saturday.

Chapter 11

Double Dipping

Chicago was on my mind. For months I had anticipated the week that now lay immediately ahead. I wasn't going to Chicago to teach a Bible school, lead singing at a revival, or teach a course at a church summer camp. Instead, the next week would be a break in my schedule of student summer service work. I put out my thumb for a ride to the 1956 Democratic National Convention, where I would attend as an alternate delegate from Alabama's Fifth Congregational District.

I had first become interested in attending a national political convention six months earlier in government class at college. In this class, we studied political parties and conventions, and I learned that the Democrats and Republicans would hold their next conventions in August. Having just turned twenty-one, which made me eligible, I decided to get myself elected as a delegate to one of the conventions. At the end of one of my classes, I stayed late to talk with the professor about my idea.

"Are you a Democrat or a Republican?" he inquired.

"I don't know."

I had never thought much about party affiliation. Practically every public official in Alabama at that time was a Democrat. At the state and local level, there was rarely any discussion about ideological differences between the Democrats and Republicans.

"If you are a Republican," my professor went on to say, "you'll have little chance of election because all delegates to their convention are chosen in a statewide conference. You will have two things against you. First, when you stand up at the conference and they see how young you are, you wouldn't have a chance. Second, the Republican organization in Alabama is a small, close-knit group. Delegates to national conventions are usually chosen from the key workers of the party. On the other hand, if you're a Democrat, you'll have a chance to be elected because all of their delegates are chosen in the primaries. You can get your name on the ballot and stand as good a chance to be elected as the next fellow for two reasons: one, your age won't be against you because no one can tell your age from looking at the ballot. Two, candidates for delegate positions do practically no campaigning."

"I'm a Democrat," I announced. "What do we do next?"

"Laugh!" he chuckled. And we did.

In the days following, we decided my chances for election would be best if I qualified for an alternate delegate position from my home district, the Fifth Congressional District in East Alabama. Sixteen delegates and sixteen alternates were to be elected from the state at large. Each of the nine congressional districts would elect four delegates and two alternates. We figured the least contested position would be an alternate position from my district.

From my standpoint, an alternate position was satisfactory. I would have full convention privileges, including the right of debate. My only limitation would be lack of voting privileges. Also, I would have the chance of becoming a full delegate, including voting privileges, if one of our district delegates became incapacitated or had to leave the convention.

I wrote the secretary of state of Alabama for the necessary qualifying papers, filled them out, returned them with the $10.00 qualifying fee, and anxiously waited for the deadline to pass so I could see who my "opponents" were.

When the list of all candidates for all positions in the Democratic primary were printed in the newspapers in early April, I was overjoyed to see that only two people—myself and one other man—had qualified for the two alternate delegate positions from the Fifth District. I had won my first election without a contest!

For the remainder of the spring and all summer, I received a steady stream of material about the convention. I filled my head with facts about candidates and issues. Dozens of letters came from the

Democratic National Committee about issues and fundraising. Books, brochures, booklets, and letters came from aspiring candidates.

As I started my hitchhiking trek toward Chicago, I was filled with a tremendous sense of excitement and a feeling of responsibility. I had started on this adventure out of curiosity and interest, but a summer of studying the problems facing the Democratic party made me feel a part of what was about to happen. I wanted to be a good delegate; I wanted to do a good job at the convention. And I was anxious to get to Chicago for another reason—to see a girlfriend.

Four years earlier, while attending the National Junior Achievement Conference at Valley Forge, Pennsylvania, I had met Bonnie Wahlstrom, a J. A. delegate from Chicago. I fell head over heels in love with her. I thought she was the prettiest, sweetest girl I had ever met. We had a teenage conference romance, complete with moonlight strolls in a rose garden, a gala conference-ending ball on the last night of the week, and a park bench kiss afterward to celebrate her sixteenth birthday.

After that, we corresponded furiously, and when I went off to college I hitchhiked up to see her every chance I got.

In recent months, though, she had not been answering my letters promptly. I was worried.

On previous visits to Chicago, I had stayed in the Wahlstroms' home. This time, however, I had made arrangements to be a guest in the home of John Faulstich, national president of the Youth Fellowship of the Evangelical and Reformed Church. He lived in Gary, Indiana. I didn't stay with John for long. On my first trip from his home into the city, I called Bonnie and invited her to meet me at the Palmer Hotel, where a party was underway. Jim Folsom, governor of Alabama, was giving the party for all the Alabama delegates. She met me there, and in the whirlwind of the convention and party atmosphere, our past differences evaporated.

The next day, I moved in with the Wahlstroms in Chicago for the remainder of the week. I had one of the grandest times of my life! Every minute of the convention was filled with excitement, and Bonnie was with me to fill every minute of my free time.

I met many famous people: Bull Conner, Frank Clement, John Kennedy, Estes Kefauver, Happy Chandler, and George Wallace (who at the time was unknown outside Alabama).

One of the books I had received and read during the summer was about Estes Kefauver. I remembered from the book that Mr. Kefauver had a "phenomenal" memory. It said if he had ever met anyone, he never forgot that person. I was on an elevator one day when Mr. Kefauver stepped in. I extended my hand and introduced myself. We conversed until he left the elevator. A couple of days later, I was at a reception with Bonnie. Mr. Kefauver was in the receiving line.

"Mr. Kefauver, this is Bonnie Wahlstrom."

"Hello, Mrs. Wahlstrom," he said with a broad smile. And, looking at me, he boomed, "How are you, Mr. Walhstrom?"

He was human all right. But I still voted for him as our vice-presidential nominee later in the week.

As a matter of fact, I almost got in a fight trying to vote for him. About the middle of the week, one of our delegates had to leave the convention. By the convention rules, I was first alternate so I automatically became a full delegate, filling his vacancy. When the Alabama delegation caucused to nominate a vice-president, the secretary began calling the roll of delegates to receive their vote. When he came to the name of the delegate for whom I was alternate, he didn't call it. I realized he did not intend to call it, so I stood and called for his attention. He would not look up. I jumped into my chair and yelled for him to stop the proceeding until my vote was recorded. Every time he attempted to call out another name I interrupted him. Shortly, one of the secretary's aides started toward me, shaking his fist and angrily demanding that I shut up and sit down. I didn't move.

Just before he reached me, a couple of fellow delegates rushed to my defense. (One of those men was Ralph Williams of Tuscaloosa, Alabama. I moved into his house when I entered the University of Alabama Law School a year later.) The aide sheepishly turned around and headed back up front. My new friends took up my cause. In a matter of seconds others stood with me. The secretary, by now pale faced, called for my vote. I yelled out "Estes Kefauver," and the caucus continued.

Those caucuses were always a thrill. When we met earlier to nominate a presidential candidate, for instance, dozens of people made speeches about various candidates. At the last minute, Frank Clement, then governor of Tennessee, walked in wearing a ten-gallon hat and made a short, fiery speech on behalf of Albert Gore, Sr., senator from his state. Then he sat down. Without any debate, we voted unanimously to yield to Tennessee so they could nominate Albert Gore. Prior to Governor Clement's speech, Gore had not been mentioned!

I was one of the youngest delegates at the convention and the only one who hitchhiked to get there. I was interviewed one morning on the TV show *Today*. On another occasion, I told of my hitchhiking experiences on a radio program sponsored by Governor "Happy" Chandler of Kentucky.

The entire week in Chicago was packed with everything but sleep. Some nights I got to bed at three or four o'clock and rose in the morning at seven o'clock. Only the excitement of it all kept me going.

Chapter 12

On and Off Campus

It all caught up with me the next week in Salisbury, North Carolina.

After the 1956 Democratic Convention ended, I hitchhiked across country to Catawba College in Salisbury, where I was to attend the National Youth Conference of the Evangelical and Reformed Church. I had been selected as one of four young people from the Congregational Christian Church to be a fraternal delegate to their national conference. The next year, the two denominations would conclude a merger to form the United Church of Christ.

I caught a ride in Ohio with a man going to Wheeling, West Virginia. We entered that little town past midnight. He let me out and pulled away, leaving me on the loneliest, quietest road I have ever seen. I stood out there for about an hour, and not a single car came by. I was exhausted. I started to walk. In a few minutes, I spotted an old school bus parked in a vacant lot just off the road. I walked over, pried the front door open, climbed in, and sprawled out on the long back seat.

It was broad daylight the next morning when I awakened. I staggered out, raised my thumb on a now busy highway, and soon was on my way again to Salisbury.

It was sheer torture trying to stay awake the next week. My nodding in conference sessions became a joke. In spite of that, however, I had a great time there. It was a perfect climax to a tremendous summer.

At the week's end, I thumbed my way south to my home in Lanett and started thinking about my senior year of college at Auburn University.

I had entered Auburn in fall 1953. At first, I was in the School of Agriculture, studying agricultural engineering. I had thought I could combine my interest in business with my interest in cattle and farming. It didn't work out, though, so I changed to an economics major at the end of my sophomore year.

Auburn University is in East Alabama in the little town of Auburn. When I was there, it was known as Auburn Polytechnic Institute. As in all of Alabama, everyone is nuts about football. At Auburn, the school spirit seems to improve as the football team deteriorates. It matters little how many games are won or lost during the season. The year is a great success if the University of Alabama, a land-grant college in Tuscaloosa, is defeated in the last game of the season.

While at Auburn, I occasionally wrote for the school paper and was engaged in numerous other extracurricular pursuits, both on the campus and elsewhere. During my freshman year, I played on the varsity baseball team. I was a left-handed pitcher. I didn't get to pitch much, but the prospect was bright that I would pitch often the following year. I had been an avid baseball player; before college I had played on both high school and American Legion teams. In one game I had pitched a no-hitter, beating Talladega, Alabama, 20-0! My picture was in the paper and I was the hero of the town for a few days.

After my freshman baseball season at Auburn ended in the spring, I joined a semi-professional team in my hometown of Lanett for the summer baseball season. In July, I pitched at a St. Louis Cardinal tryout camp in Columbus, Georgia. The scout spoke encouragingly after the tryout and said he wanted to talk to me after my next year at Auburn. That never came to pass. Shortly after the tryout camp, I left for a couple of weeks to attend the National Pilgrim Fellowship Conference at Yale University. The day after I returned from the conference, I pitched a full nine-inning game. This proved to be my undoing. My arm was not in condition to pitch, and I developed a severe pain in my shoulder. It never left me. I went out for the varsity team the next year, but my shoulder hurt so badly I could hardly throw the ball the distance from mound to plate. I voluntarily gave up my uniform before the regular season started. Thus ended my baseball career.

It was just as well. There were more than enough other activities to fill the void.

Chapter 13

Ever Ready

Beginning in fall 1954—my sophomore year at Auburn—I worked in nearby Opelika as program director of a new Junior Achievement program in that city. I held the position for the next three years. The first year of operation we had four little J.A. companies. Two met on Tuesday nights, and the other two met on Thursday nights. In ensuing years we had six companies, with two each night—Mondays, Tuesdays, and Thursdays. I hitchhiked the seven miles to Opelika late in the afternoon and returned the same way about 9:30 in the evening for three school years.

On weekends, I traveled throughout the southeast for Pilgrim Fellowship or went home to Lanett, where on Sunday I taught a Sunday school class in my home church. In my entire college career at Auburn, I spent less than three weekends on campus. This created a void in my college experience that I regret. I worked most evenings during the week in Opelika and was gone on weekends. When could I have a date or go to a party? In four years at Auburn, I think I had five or six dates with Auburn girls.

This void in my college experience cost me in a specific way during my junior year. I had become interested in campus politics through the War Eagle Political Party and the Auburn Independent organization. I was president of the latter group, which represented the non-fraternity students on campus, for two years, and had been a founding member of the War Eagle Party in my freshman year. Prior to the organization of this party, there was only one party on campus, the All-Campus Party. It was controlled by a certain group of fraternities and sororities with no representation from the non-Greek students.

In spring of my freshman year, I ran for the student senate on this party ticket. I lost. In the following two years, I served on various committees, wrote some for the student paper, joined with fellow student William Callahan to win a campus-wide debate tournament, and did other things to become known around campus. In my junior year, the War Eagle Party selected me as the party's first candidate to run for president of the student government association.

I nearly worked myself sick trying to win that job. I spoke more than seventy times during a period of thirty days. I visited every dormitory and most of the fraternities and sororities. We put huge signs on top of dozens of cars and parked them in strategic places all over campus. Groups of supporters were organized to parade around campus with signs on long sticks. Cards were handed out at all buildings at every break between classes. Some girls in the party sewed jackets for all dogs on campus with lettering on the sides proclaiming "Fuller for President!"

On election day, everybody I saw told me I was a shoo-in to win and that the other fellow running didn't have a chance. I was sure, too, that I would win. In fact, I wondered if my opponent would get any votes! As I crawled in bed the night of the election, visions of sugarplums danced in my head. On the morrow I would be president of the Student Government Association. But, surprise of all surprises, I lost! When I learned I was defeated, I was too sick to live. I was crushed. I wanted to go off in the woods somewhere, crawl in a log, and die! I felt that way once before when I learned I had made an "F" in an integral calculus course. Then I wanted to jump off a building. I came close in this election. Out of a total of 3700 votes cast, I got 1600. But, in an election, the second man gets nothing. Don't ever go into politics unless you are prepared for the greatest of heartbreaks.

When I recovered enough from the shock of my unexpected loss, I analyzed the voting. The male students voted for me. I carried the schools of Veterinary Medicine, Agriculture, and Engineering. The women did not vote for me. I lost in the schools of Education, Science, and Literature and others with large concentrations of women students. I should have done my social "homework" on weekends!

My summers were as busy as my weeknights and weekends during days at Auburn. The summer of 1956, my student summer service assignments were exciting and rewarding. But the summer of 1955 had been quite a different kind of adventure.

The summer of 1955 (before my junior year at Auburn) started in Flint, Michigan. I went there at the beginning with a fellow Auburnite who lived in the city. He thought I could get employment in one of the automobile factories. I desired the experience work in a large factory would offer, but I also wanted and needed the money for school.

From the beginning of college, I had earned my own way. Even before entering college, I had made money selling rabbits, pigs, and cows. The summer after my junior year in high school, I worked in the Lanett Bleachery and Dye Works on the third shift—11:00 p.m. until 7:00 a.m. They called this the "graveyard shift." If you have ever worked such hours, you know why. I went to sleep walking around one night and crashed head first into a steel post. In the mornings that summer, I trapped and seined for minnows in country branches and creeks. My dad and I dug a little pool beside his store and sold the minnows to local fishermen. I didn't mind working.

Once in Flint, I made the rounds to all the plants—to Buick, AC Spark Plug, and others. A couple of days went by and still no job. I took off for Detroit.

My aunt Avis, one of my mother's sisters, lived there with her husband and family. She had come south back when I was twelve, and I returned with her on a train. After a two-week visit, I returned home alone on the train, even changing trains in Cincinnati. I will never forget how huge that station looked and how little I felt! Aunt Avis had wanted me to return for another visit, so I made her place my home while searching for a job. On my second day out, I landed one at the Gemmer Steering Gear factory. I went to work on the second shift—3:00 p.m. until 11:00 p.m. My job was to operate a drill press. The men on my right would hand me a gear mechanism, which I placed under a drill press. I pulled the handle down, drilled out a little hole, then passed it to the man on my left for him to drill a hole somewhere else. It definitely was not the most interesting job I'd ever had!

A few days later, I found a second job. I became a door-to-door salesman of ladies' hosiery and undergarments for Real Silk Hosiery Company. I did my selling in the mornings and early afternoons and then went to work at Gemmer Steering Gear. This second job was anything but boring. Dogs chased me, ladies poured out their hearts to me about marital problems, and I sold bloomers and stockings! My "pitch" at the door went something like this: "Hello, I'm Millard Fuller, your Real Silk representative, and I'd like to step inside and show you . . . ."

"Who'd you say you were with?" most would ask. "The Fuller Brush Company?"

"No, Real Silk Hosiery." Then I spent the next few minutes clearing up my identity.

This experience taught me about the psychology of selling. At the beginning of the job, I received a one-day training session. I was told to ring the doorbell and immediately move back, well away from the door. If possible, I was to stand on the steps at a level lower than the housewife. I learned that standing close to the door on an equal or higher elevation would often startle the woman and make her suspicious. The chances of getting her confidence and a sale greatly diminished. I learned to stand with my best facial and body profile facing the door. This was the "first impression" I was taught to present to my potential customers.

Once a customer opened the door, I was to smile, speak in pleasant tones, and move slowly, with deliberation, toward the door. This encouraged the housewife to invite me inside.

I was taught, and learned it to be true, that few sales are made at the door. It is crucial to the success of a door-to-door salesman to get inside. For one thing, people are seldom curt or rude inside their homes. They will insult you, even curse you, while you are outside, but once they let you in, they are nice. When I made it over the threshold, I tried to change the subject immediately. I found something to compliment. A cute baby. A nice dog. A lovely cat. Pretty flowers. Beautiful furniture. Anything.

Finally, I got back on the subject of Real Silk Hosiery goods. I took out a box and began talking about its contents, holding it as if it contained something precious. The object of the game was to keep talking long enough to make the lady of the house want to see what was in the box. Hopefully, and it usually worked this way, she would ask to see the contents. At that point I was responding to her desire to know about my products. The battle was half won.

On weekends, I hitchhiked around the state. On one trip, I went all the way to Sault St. Marie and back to Detroit in one day. I actually went to the Straits of Mackinaw seeking employment on the bridge that was then under construction. At the Straits, I was told I'd have to go on to Sault St. Marie because the Union Temple that cleared employees for the bridge was located there. Upon arriving in Sault Ste. Marie, I found that a party was underway in the Union Temple. I couldn't get anyone interested in talking to me about work on the bridge. So, being only half-heartedly interested in that kind of work, I turned around and thumbed my way back to Detroit.

Just before the week of July 4, I got "laid off" at Gemmer Steering Gear. The foreman said I'd probably be rehired in a couple of weeks, but I did not want to wait. The Real Silk job was not making enough money to justify spending full time on it. Anyway, I was restless and wanted to work somewhere else.

I told my aunt good-bye and thumbed my way to Chicago. The first day there, I got a job with Goldblatt's Department Store. I worked out of their big warehouse as a helper on a furniture delivery truck. My driver was a big Polish fellow named Mike. He was a man of few words. Most of what he said was peppered with epitaphs of varying degrees of vulgarity. His temper was terrible. As we drove around on our deliveries, he would curse every car, truck, or pedestrian that got in his way. I was constantly amazed that he was not physically attacked by some of the people who heard him.

I worked on the truck with Mike for most of July. One day we were driving along, and out of the blue he asked why I didn't curse. I simply shared with him my feeling that it was inconsistent with the way God wants man to live. "Man," I continued, "was not created to yell and scream at each other and curse everyone who gets in our way."

Mike was pensive the rest of that day and cursed very little. The next day, though, he was back at it again.

It seemed that most of our deliveries were on third floors or higher. We climbed rickety stairs and struggled and strained from morning until night. If there is anything that should make a man curse, I suppose it is this kind of work.

When I left Goldblatt's at the month's end, Mike and I had become good friends. I worked with him again during Christmas holiday that year.

About August 1, I hitchhiked back to Detroit and the next day to Flint, Michigan, where I worked for the remaining months of the summer.

When I arrived in Flint, I rented a room in an old downtown hotel. I stayed there for a week. Then I went looking for a cheaper place in a private home. Looking in a newspaper, I spotted an inexpensive room not far from where I worked. I went to the address one evening and looked over the place. It seemed satisfactory. I paid the lady for a week in advance and moved in. The next morning, I came downstairs for breakfast. When I started to sit on the living room sofa, a little girl yelled, "Don't sit there. You'll get flea powder on you!" It had begun. That place was miserable. The woman entertained men at night. The house was a wreck and a constant circus. I had arrived the night before at a rare quiet time and looked over the house when lighting was dim. I was too tight on money to move out early and sustain a loss. The instant my week was up, I left to find better quarters. My next room was much nicer, and I lived there for the remainder of my time in peace and quiet.

I had two jobs in Flint. My first was with a bakery. I got it through the State Employment Office and worked with two other men unloading flour from a railroad car onto a flat-bed truck. We then drove across town and unloaded it at the bakery. My coworkers on this job were characters. Both were alcoholics. One lived in his car. The other man, called "Boots," lived in a cave on the river. We got paid at the end of every day. By the next morning, both of these men were broke, having spent every penny on whiskey and other items during the night. They borrowed money from me for lunch and paid me back in the evening. "Boots" was a preacher. All day he quoted the Bible and orated. Especially on our trips across town with a load of flour, he held forth with great vigor. I was always surprised at how these men could keep up a hard pace of work all day in spite of the enormous amounts of alcohol they consumed each night.

My second job was with a small company that erected prefabricated houses. It was vigorous outside work, and I loved it. Within a few days, I had a deep tan, and, as we say in the South, I felt as "strong as a mule." My closest companion on this job was a young man named Bob. He was long on friendliness and talking and short on brains and memory. It was impossible, for instance, for him to remember the name of even close friends. He called everybody "Shorty." That wouldn't have been too bad except for the fact that he was constantly yelling out "Hey, Shorty, do this or that, come here, go there," etcetera. Every worker had to look up when he yelled "Shorty." I decided to remedy the situation as far as I was concerned. I called him aside and said, "Bob, my name is not 'Shorty.' It is Millard. Now, I'm going to tell you how you can remember that. Have you ever heard of a Willard battery?"

"Yes," he replied.

"Okay," I said. "When you want to call me, first think of a battery. Then think of Willard. Last of all, turn the "W" upside down. That'll make 'Millard.' Call me by that name."

"All right," he muttered as he walked away.

He was silent for a while and then he yelled out, "Hey, Shorty . . . I mean . . . hey, you!" Out of the corner of my eye I could see that he was calling me, but I wouldn't look up. He continued.

"Okay, I know your name has something to do with a battery. Is your name 'EverReady'?"

Many times since then I have used this little incident in talks. It always brings peals of laughter from any audience.

In early September, I bought a secondhand Plymouth automobile with part of my earnings and drove south to Alabama, thus bringing to a close my "work-travel" summer. As always, I was "ever ready" for the next adventure.

1932—Estin Cook and
Render Fuller

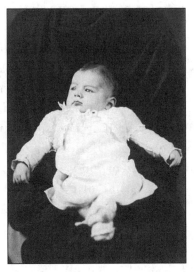

1935—Millard 3 months.

2007—Millard in front of the house where he
was born in Lanett, Alabama

1937—Millard with parents,
Estin and Render Fuller

1938—Millard standing on
mother's grave.

1937—Millard standing with father at a church
gathering. Estin, second woman from right.

1941—Millard, age 6

1941—Millard, from an early
age, was fascinated with
snakes and other wildlife.

1939—Millard sitting on hood
of family automobile.

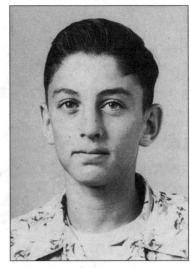

1945—Millard, 10 years

Millard (right, dressed in overalls and with bare feet)—
5th grade class at Huguley Elementary School.

Millard's favorite primary teacher, Mrs. Talley, standing
with 6th grade class of 1946–1947. (Reason unknown
why Millard has been removed from photo directly
over Mrs. Talley)

1953—Millard, the talented
left-handed baseball pitcher.

1952—Render and Eunice showing off one of
the fine cows at their farm.

1954—Millard, 19 years   1956—Millard, age 21

Summer 1955—Planning Committee of
Southeast Conference of Congregational
Church (Millard, second from right).

March 20, 1955—Millard (middle
with light suit) is president of
Southeast Conference of
Pilgrim Fellowship.

Pilgrim Fellowship delegates
at New Haven: Albert Van
Cleave, Betty Slater,
Millard Fuller.

1955 Pilgrim Fellowship of Southeast Conference of Congregational
Church (Rev. Annie Campbell, far right)

1956—Millard, Alabama delegate to the National Democratic
Convention in Chicago.

Part 2

Building the Dream

(1957–1964)

Chapter 14

My Own Business

One Christmas while a student at Auburn, I became involved in an exciting and profitable enterprise with Donald Moore, a fellow Auburn student and a distant cousin. We discovered that the trees on Auburn's campus were loaded with mistletoe. After receiving permission to cut it, we rigged up sharp hooks on long canes and started clipping the mistletoe. We loaded my car and drove first to Montgomery to sell a load, then to Birmingham, and finally to Chattanooga.

As we were returning home from our first trip to Montgomery, the car in front of us stopped suddenly. Donald, who was driving, slammed on brakes. As we came to a screeching halt, we heard a squealing of brakes and then, "Wham!" My nice car I bought in Flint was never the same after that. Fortunately, the car behind us swerved enough to avoid hitting us straight on. The only damage done to my car was a torn left rear fender. The car that hit us was a total wreck. We kicked the fender back somewhat into shape and drove back to Auburn.

Our day of selling mistletoe was good, but I felt sick about my car. A few days later, my feelings improved when I collected more than a hundred dollars—worth a couple thousand in the 1950s—from the insurance company of the other car for damages to my car. I put the money in my pocket and left the fender like it was. The car would still run, and that was all I cared about.

The next Christmas—my senior year at Auburn—I loaded my dad's car with mistletoe (I was afraid mine wouldn't make the trip) and drove to Chicago. I knew the price would be higher there, and I wanted to see Bonnie. After selling the mistletoe, I worked the remaining days of Christmas vacation for Goldblatt's Department Store before returning south for the last few months of college.

Without a doubt, my college career had been full. For three years I had packed in as much as I possibly could—days, nights, weekends, vacations, and summers. I always had something going. I had heard and believed that youth is the time to do something and become somebody. My aim was to fill my life with as many varied experiences as time allowed. All the while, I had a sense of being close to God and in tune with his reality—or will—for my life.

My senior year at Auburn was filled with serious study. Even though I continued my work with Junior Achievement and organized and served as president of a campus Young Democrats club, my main focus was attending classes and preparing for examinations. I was thinking deeply about my future. Always there had been another year of school. But what about next year?

I began to interview with companies for possible positions. Babcock and Wilcox Company invited me to New York. They offered a job, but I turned it down. I talked with Creole Petroleum Company about a job in Caracus, Venezuela, but that really didn't excite me either. I didn't want to get a job with some big company and spend the rest of my life "climbing the ladder" to top leadership. My ideas about going into business didn't include this avenue.

Rev. Annie Campbell and several others encouraged me to go to seminary to prepare for the ministry. I seriously considered it but realized I did not feel led in that direction. The preaching part of the ministry did not bother me. I felt I could do that and enjoy it. What I thought I could not tolerate was the bickering and constant friction that goes on in many churches.

One day I was sitting in the Student Union Building, and a fellow student, Jim Gullage, walked over and sat down.

"How about going to law school with me?

"Good idea," I replied. "How do we get in?"

Then he told me he would soon be going to the university campus in Tuscaloosa to take the Law School Aptitude Test. I quickly agreed to go with him. Even though, at that time, I had no particular desire to practice law, I figured a law degree would be helpful in either a business or political career—and maybe in other areas too. I was fired up about politics since going to the Democratic Convention, and I had long been interested in business.

I graduated from Auburn on June 4, 1957, and entered the University of Alabama Law School six days later—on June 10.

Chapter 15

Meeting My Match

Law school was tough! I thought I'd been studying a lot at Auburn, but I was yet to learn the real meaning of the word "study." I became a virtual recluse that first semester. The law school used the "case method" of teaching law. Every day the class was assigned various law cases to read. The next day in class, various students were called on at random to recite the facts of the case, give points of law raised, and discussed all issues. The pace was grueling. When I entered law school, I had 20-20 vision without glasses. By midpoint of my law school career, I was bespectacled. The overwhelming majority of law students are "speckled," too, due to hours of required reading.

When I arrived on campus, I was almost broke. Money I had made on rabbits, pigs, cattle, and other enterprises had been consumed in my years at Auburn. I barely had enough for tuition and books. No money remained for food. I got a job as a waiter at Sandusky's Boarding House. My pay was my meals and $50 a month.

A few weeks later, I took a second job of milking cows for Ma Britton's Boarding House to get a little extra money. Ma Britton had a boarding house for students across the street from Sandusky's. She had her own brood of cows on a farm at the edge of town, and students did the milking.

By mid-summer, I was beginning to worry about my finances for the fall semester and future semesters. In the past, I had been interested in making money, but not for reasons of necessity. I had always had money in the bank. Not anymore. I was down to a hand-to-mouth existence with no reserves except possibly a loan from my dad, and I didn't want to ask him because his funds were low. Where and how could I get money for my upcoming expenses?

The answer was not long in coming.

One day at law school I saw a notice on the bulletin board of a summer meeting of the University Young Democrats. It was to be held at the Student Union Building. I hadn't been to a single movie or gone on a date since arriving on campus. I was interested in the Young Democrats, however, so I decided to attend.

After my last class was dismissed that afternoon, I went to my room and started studying. I pored over the assigned cases and "briefed" them for the next day. By late afternoon, I was finished with my homework. I ran to the boarding house, ate a quick meal, washed some dishes, and raced to the Student Union Building.

As I approached the meeting room of the Young Democrats, a student I did not know greeted me. He extended his hand.

"My name is Morris Dees," he said. "I'm running for secretary of the Young Democrats and I'd like your vote."

I explained that I had arrived at the university only a few weeks prior and that I was not yet a member of the chapter. We talked briefly and I walked in to find a seat.

In a few minutes, the president of the group called the meeting to order. The young man I met at the door walked up the aisle and took a seat beside me.

After a routine meeting, my new friend walked outside with me. We stood in the warm night air for a few minutes talking about college, Young Democrats, and other things. Finally, I turned to walk away.

"How are you traveling?" he inquired.

"I'm walking."

"Get in my car, then, and I'll drive you to your place."

We got in his car. I was living that summer in the home of Ralph Williams, the delegate who had jumped to my defense at the Democratic National Convention in Chicago the previous summer. He was a lawyer in Tuscaloosa.

By the time we reached the house, our conversation was no longer about school and politics. We were talking business. Dees, I quickly discovered, had much in common with me. He had been reared on a farm near Montgomery, Alabama. He was interested in politics. He had raised cattle and engaged in various enterprises as a schoolboy. And he had long dreamed of developing some kind of business. He loved promoting and selling. We spoke a common language.

For a few minutes after stopping the car, he left the motor running, but soon he turned it off. We had a lot to discuss.

He told me about some of his recent enterprises: selling rotten cotton burrs to homeowners for spreading around shrubbery and flowers and selling lists of names of college seniors to insurance companies. Also, he told me about his idea of selling cypress knees for decorative pieces in homes. Cypress knees are root appendages on the bald cypress trees that abound in South Alabama and Florida. I told him my project of selling mistletoe at Auburn and about my idea of selling it in quantity through florist shops. We tossed ideas around on how our various projects could expand and how we could develop a profitable business from them. On and on we talked. Before either of us realized it, the time was 2:00 a.m.!

We decided to work together in developing and promoting our two ideas of selling mistletoe and cypress knees. We agreed that we couldn't fail if we got something for nothing and sold it for a big price. In that way, most of our sales would be pure profit. We laughed at the motto that came rolling off the top of our heads: "To Get Rich."

I reached across and grasped Morris's hand. We shook and said goodnight. Our business was born.

Chapter 16

Miserable Failures

I had known Morris Dees for less than eight hours, and we were in business together. For the next eight years, we were almost inseparable companions. We said millions of words to each other in thousands of such talk-a-thons. We worked hard together and did things over and over that most people said couldn't be done. Fellow students, family, and friends laughed at us, but we built up a million-dollar business within six years on our "crazy" ideas.

Indeed, as a freshman law student, I would soon solve my money problems. I was on the road to becoming a millionaire. I did not know it then, but the course of my life was changed in Morris Dees's car that night.

Dees was a junior in the School of Commerce. He planned to enter law school a year later. I was deeply impressed with his enthusiasm and vibrant personality. I had never met anyone with such quick and deep perception. His mind was fertile and creative. During our years together in business, he was usually the "idea" man who thought up the next project. One word about an idea, and he had the whole concept. Later, we were able to talk the equivalent of five hours in one or two words. His concentration was intense. Not a muscle moved when he heard an idea explained. The same intensity was present when he shared something. He was eager, aggressive, and positive when engaged in discussing anything, but especially when talking about business and selling and making money. Physically, he was trim and vigorous. He was the personification of a Spartan athlete. About six feet tall, he had smooth features and short wavy blonde hair. Indeed, no one in my life had ever made such a positive impression on me.

As I stumbled into bed that first night, I was happy about my new friend and about what we had planned during the evening.

In the days and weeks that followed, we saw a lot of each other and talked a great deal more about our idea, especially the mistletoe and cypress knees.

Our new company, we decided, would simply be called "Fuller and Dees." A little later, when we decided to sell the cypress knees, we renamed the company "Fuller and Dees Heart of Dixie Products." We thought this was a better name for selling such "southern" items. After college, we dropped "Heart of Dixie." At that time, because of racial problems in the South, we felt "Heart of Dixie" was a liability to a company with customers throughout the nation. We were always changing the name of the company, adding new ventures, and operating them under other names. At various times during the next eight years, we had company names such as Bama Cake Service; Home-Ec Press; Favorite Recipes Press, Inc.; Outstanding Young Americans, Inc.; Athletic Publishing Company; Color Litho, Inc.; Fuller and Dees, Inc.; Dees and Fuller Marketing Group, Inc.; Fuller and Dees Farm; Fuller Fund Raising Company; The Fuller Company; and Off to College, Inc. We never were in short supply of company names! If a new product or idea did not fit into an existing company, we thought up a new one!

In early fall, we decided to send out a mailing to test our mistletoe idea. We secured a Floral Telegraph Delivery Book and addressed envelopes to about 300 florists. We composed a letter that read, "We have mistletoe for sale. The price is $.40 a pound. How many pounds would you like to order?" We dropped these letters in the mail. Within two weeks, we had orders for more than 3,000 pounds of mistletoe!

We were ecstatic. I could see all that money in the bank. I didn't expect success so quickly.

But then a sudden realization hit us: we didn't have 3,000 pounds of mistletoe. We didn't have even one pound! When I had sold it at Auburn, it was by the piece or by the box—never by the pound. We decided we had better check the weight of mistletoe. We went out and clipped a large box of it from a tree on campus. You can imagine our dismay when we discovered it only weighed one pound!

We weren't about to give up. We had orders for 3,000 pounds, and we wanted to fill them. On weekends we traveled around the state looking for 3,000 pounds of mistletoe. We went everywhere and talked to wholesale florists and others we thought might help with the problem. We never found the mistletoe. Our first venture was a total failure. We wrote our new customers a "letter of regret and apologies," and we went out of the mistletoe business.

At the same time we were testing our mistletoe idea, we were hard at work on the cypress knees. We rented a tiny building near the university campus. In it, we built a homemade furnace and boiler. The boiler was for cooking the cypress knees so we could remove the bark, leaving a smooth surface. My dad loaned us his truck so we could haul the knees up to the campus on weekends. By October, we were deep into the production of cypress knees.

We designed and printed a brochure extolling the virtues of our "knees." "Cypress Knees by Fuller and Dees"; "Southern Beauty Designed by Nature," "The Story of the Cypress Knee": these captions announced our unusual product on the cover of our advertising piece. Inside, we continued,

> From the Deep Swamps of the Deep South . . . Cypress Knees . . . Nature's own creation of modern art . . . are yours to be enjoyed . . . .
>
> Cypress Knees are odd-shaped appendages that project upward above the dark swampy water from the roots of the bald Cypress tree. Through a special process of removing the bark, the wood surface retains its own natural velvet-smooth finish. The wood color ranges from dusk tan to rawhide brown. Each knee is a work of art . . . a Jewel of Beauty . . . .
>
> There are hundreds of uses for Cypress Knees . . . limited only by a creative mind. . . . From the workshop to a modern home. Heart of Dixie Cypress Knees create beauty and stimulate compliments . . . .

Law school did not get any easier, but I learned to budget my time more carefully and sleep a little less. On a typical day during this period, I attended classes in the morning and early afternoon. Then, in the late afternoon, I briefed all cases for the next day. After supper, Dees and I met at our little building to boil and peel cypress knees. After completing this operation, we had to square off the bottoms on an electric saw we had rigged. Finally, they had to be placed on racks in the back of the building so the sun would dry them.

To our sorrow, three unfortunate incidents happened in our cypress knee business. First, we found out that an acid under the bark of the cypress knee caused the skin to peel off our hands. It became difficult for us to write. Second, we wrecked my father's truck. Dees was bringing in a load of cypress knees one day and turned left just as a woman decided to pass. The left side of my father's truck took on a rugged appearance after that encounter. He wasn't too happy about the new look, but he didn't ask us to have it fixed. Third, we discovered that the cost of getting each cypress knee ready to sell was high. When we priced them in order to realize a profit, no one bought them. One of the factors that raised the cost was the fact that the cypress knees wouldn't dry fast enough in the sun. We eventually had to put them in a drying kiln at a lumberyard.

Before Christmas, we came to the conclusion that our cypress knee idea wasn't going to work. It took us several more months to get out of this business as we tried to recoup some of our expenses. Among other things, we attempted to make lamps out of the knees, but they were so light that they wouldn't stand up. We made a long drill to bore a hole through the knees for the electric cord to pass through. One night a friend was helping us with drilling. The drill came loose and ripped his face open. We ended up giving away hundreds of cypress knees and throwing hundreds of others in the city dump. Our second venture was a failure.

By this time I was not only broke, but I was deeply in debt. Dees had saved money from earlier ventures, and we had used his funds to finance the new business. But now he was broke, too. Our backs were against the wall. There is an old saying that "necessity is the mother of invention." We were at the threshold of testing this axiom.

Chapter 17

Turning the Tide

While searching for mistletoe earlier in the fall, we had gone to Evergreen, Alabama, to see Knud Nielsen, president of the Knud Nielsen Wholesale Florist Company. We had walked in that day and introduced ourselves.

"We're looking for 3,000 pounds of mistletoe," we announced.

"You're what?" he retorted.

Then we explained what we had done. He almost fell out of his seat laughing.

He admonished us to give up the search because, in his opinion, what we were searching for was impossible to get. As an alternate idea, he suggested that we sell imported Italian holly wreaths to youth groups for fundraising purposes. He explained that a Boy Scout troop in Texas had ordered from him the year before and that they had sold the wreaths like "hot cakes." We asked a few questions about the wreaths, but we eventually rejected the idea because we were sure at the time that we could somehow get the mistletoe.

Now, however, it was November, and our two great ideas—mistletoe and cypress knees—were in shambles. Fuller and Dees needed a winner. We decided to call Mr. Nielsen to see if he would supply us with wreaths if we could get a group to sell them. His answer was a quick "yes."

Dees went to the local executive of the Boy Scouts and got his permission to call a meeting of the area Scoutmasters to discuss the possibility of a holly wreath sale in Tuscaloosa and the surrounding area. The local Calvary Baptist Church gave us permission to use their fellowship hall for the meeting. We carefully planned to discuss the "how" of a sale and never to bring up the question of whether they would do it or not.

Our plan worked beautifully. Letters and phone calls got almost all of the Scoutmasters to the meeting. When they left, they had complete plans on how to sell thousands of holly wreaths. We would place wreaths on consignment with each Scout troop. They would sell them for $2.50 each and pay us $2.00 for each one. The remaining ones would be returned. We called Mr. Nielsen again and told him what we had done.

"We need 5,000 holly wreaths. When can you have them here?"

"Right away."

We made arrangements to keep the wreaths in a vacant grocery store. I'll never forget the afternoon our wreaths arrived in an 18-wheeler. The truck was packed full from front to back. It was the biggest truck I had ever seen! To this day, I am amazed that Knud Nielsen shipped us that many wreaths on credit when both of us were dead broke and had failed at both of our first two ventures.

We got busy. The fire department helped us put a sign over main street down town: "Buy Your Holly Wreath this Christmas from the Boy Scouts." I researched the history of the use of holly at Christmas and wrote a radio program on it. Stories were released to the *Tuscaloosa News* about the sale. Every detail of the campaign was coordinated. Each Scout troop came to the vacant store at designated times to pick up their supplies of wreaths. Cash prizes were announced for top salesmen.

When the campaign ended, the Scouts had sold all but a few of the 5,000 wreaths, making $2,500.00 in the project; we made $3,750.00. Every third house in the city had one of our wreaths on their door that Christmas. The project was a smashing success.

In early December, the president of the local florist association came to see us to protest our infringement into their business. He asked us to call off the project. We refused, and a feeble attempt was made to stop us. After Christmas, this man came back to say that, much to his surprise, the florists in town had sold more wreaths that Christmas than ever before. The Boy Scout campaign had put so much emphasis on holly wreaths that everybody wanted one. Those who didn't get a Boy Scout wreath went to the local florist shops and purchased one.

As we worked on the Boy Scout holly wreath campaign, we also got ready to sell Christmas trees. We rented a couple of lots and made arrangements with a man in Mississippi to put trees on the lots on consignment. Huge signs were painted that read, "Buy Your Christmas Trees from University Students." We called the sororities and fraternities on the campus, asking them to buy trees from us. Many did.

I had traded the car I bought in Flint, Michigan, for an old Ford automobile and driven it to the university when I first came there in June. Now we needed a truck (to deliver Christmas trees) more than a car, so I traded the Ford for an old panel truck—our first "company" vehicle.

We went into the countryside and cut wild holly and smilax. On one of these forays into the country, we inadvertently went on the land of a man who had not given us permission to gather holly. We cut down great piles of his holly and hauled it to our lots. Somehow the owner discovered that we had been on his land and cut his holly. The next evening, he came to our largest lot in a rage. Dees, who was working there, had to face him. The man planned to issue a warrant for our arrest. Dees talked him out of it. Later, he told me he didn't know how he did it. He just kept talking. Finally, the man relented and became friendly. He even let us keep the holly.

We put up lights all over the lots and hired two men to work while we attended class during the day. In the evenings, we ran the lots. We also built racks for painting the smaller trees various colors, including with gold and silver.

Without a doubt, we had the best lots in town, and the business we did proved it. We sold hundreds of trees. We picked up pinecones from beneath nearby pine trees, then painted and sold them. We sold some of our cypress knees, lamps, and leftover holly wreaths from the Boy Scout sale.

We even sold chinaberries. One day we stood around laughing about all the things we were selling. One of us said, "I'll bet we can even sell those old rotten chinaberries," pointing up to a tree on the lot. I grabbed an axe and whacked off a small limb. We broke off a cluster of the berries and dipped them in a bucket of silver paint; they came out beautiful. We hung them over a wire. Soon a lady walked up and started eyeing the berries. "Why," she said, "these are beautiful, but they look like chinaberries."

"No, ma'am," replied Dees. "Those are oriental berries, only $.25 a bunch."

"I'll take them," she replied.

By Christmas Eve, we had chopped every limb off that old chinaberry tree and sold every clump for a total of $25.00! Needless to say, like the holly wreaths, our Christmas tree project was a smashing success.

When the new year came, we were full of excitement. We had money in the bank and two successes under our belts. Surely we were on our way, with several more ideas already in the works for the coming year.

Dees and I had a beautiful working relationship. We were encouraging to one another. We thought alike about promoting and selling. We took risks and we had a genuine sense of what would work and what wouldn't. I didn't mind hard work, and Dees was the hardest-working fellow I'd ever met. On top of that, he was married and had to support a wife and a son. As long as we were in business together, I never felt that he shirked his responsibility as a business partner. My main concern was that I hold up my end of the partnership.

I had a definite feeling that this business would succeed big and that it would eventually make me the millionaire I desired to be.

About this time, I made a covenant with myself and with God not to become selfish and self-centered in the process of building up a business and acquiring wealth. I don't remember the exact day of my "agreement," but I distinctly recollect sitting in the quiet of my room one evening and thinking the matter through. I said to myself, "Look, you've wanted to make money all your life, but you are also involved with the church, so you've got to work these things together. You're not going to be the stereotyped greedy rich man. You're going to be humble and sincere and generous. You're not going to crowd God out of your life in the process of building a business and making money." After that, I went about building the business with great vigor and feeling good about it.

Chapter 18

Hard Lessons

Our business grew rapidly. The sale of holly wreaths through the Tuscaloosa Boy Scouts led to a direct-mail business of selling these wreaths to other organizations—Hi-Y and Tri-Hi-Y Clubs of the YMCA, Junior Achievement, church groups, and service clubs. We made arrangements with the company in Evergreen, Alabama, to drop-ship orders we received directly to our customers. Similar arrangements were made with wreath importers in Indiana and Philadelphia. By the time we graduated from law school, wreaths were being shipped from these three points to our customers from Maine to California. We also contacted a door mat manufacturer in Nashville, Tennessee, and made arrangements for them to ship unassembled parts to Junior Achievement "companies."

We solicited orders by mail for both the wreaths and the mats. When we received an order, we immediately airmailed it to the appropriate plant for shipment. Simultaneously, we billed the customer and notified them that the shipment was on the way. A "sales packet" we developed was supplied to the selling group. It included radio and newspaper releases, sales and collection sheets, selling hints, and suggestions on how to organize the sale.

From the beginning of our direct-mail selling to groups, we had six principles to which we rigidly adhered. First, and most important, was to send a free sample of the product before asking a customer to order. The others were fast shipping; fair and competitive prices; high profit for the selling groups; prompt answer to any complaints; and a return policy that accepted all unsold merchandise. These principles always kept us in good stead with our customers and helped us build a quick reserve of good will around the country. There is little morality or business ethics in such principles. It is simply good business to deal with customers fairly. Happy and satisfied buyers of one's products make more profits for the company.

While our mail-order selling to groups and organizations grew, we worked on several other ventures. One of these was selling advertising on desk pads to merchants near four college campuses in Alabama and Georgia. On a large piece of blotter paper—the size of a small desk— we drew blocks of various sizes. In the middle of the paper, we provided spaces for football and basketball schedules. Also, we had a list of the telephone numbers of all dormitories, fraternities, and sororities. Merchants then were personally solicited to purchase the blocks of advertising space that covered the remainder of the surface. After all ads were sold, a printer was hired to print 2,000 to 3,000 copies for each college. The last step in the process was to distribute the desk pads during the first week of class in the fall to all dormitories and fraternity houses. The pads were given without cost to the students. We made a profit of $250.00 to $400.00 per college entirely on the advertising.

This desk pad business was usually easy money. One day, for instance, I went to Auburn University, sold all the advertising for a desk pad, and returned to the University of Alabama the next day. All that remained was to pay a local student $20.00 to distribute the printed pads and then collect $400.00 in profits from the advertisers.

Sometimes, though, there were problems. I was in Athens, Georgia, one summer to sell a desk pad for the University of Georgia. It was our first time to try that campus. I was having great success. By the afternoon of the second day, I had sold every advertising space except one.

I walked into a bank near the campus and asked to see the person in charge of advertising. I was ushered into an office and met my first woman bank president. "All right," she said, "sit down and tell me what you've got." I laid my desk pad in front of her and explained the plan for advertising and distribution. She was attentive and interested. She quickly decided to take my last advertising space.

I handed her a contract. She picked up a pen and started to sign. Just then, I heard the door open behind me. Peering around my chair, the president inquired, "Yes?"

"We want to talk to him," someone said.

I did not turn to look.

The bank president put the pen down and glared at me.

Why is she looking at me like that? I wondered. I looked over my shoulder. There in the doorway stood two huge policemen. As soon as my eyes met theirs, one of them repeated, "We'd like to talk to you."

I stepped just outside the president's office.

"The chief wants to see you down at headquarters. Come along with us."

"For what?" I asked.

"I don't know. He'll tell you. Come with us."

"Just a minute."

I stepped back into the president's office, hurriedly gathered my material, apologized for the intrusion to a now suspicious president, and walked out to see a police chief.

One policeman stood on my right and the other on my left. We marched through the middle of town to the police station. Everyone along the way stared at us.

As we reached police headquarters, I was more than a little concerned. Why did he want to see me? What had I done wrong?

The chief wasted no time in getting to his concern. "What are you doing in town?" he asked.

"I'm selling spaces for a desk pad. I am a college student from the University of Alabama going around to various colleges and selling ad space to merchants. Here, let me show you the desk pad I am working on." I spread it out in front of him and explained the deal.

After I completed my explanation, he inquired further, "When do you collect the money from the merchants?"

"After the desk pad is distributed to the students in September." I showed him the signed contracts from the merchants.

He sat back and smiled. "Well, you're okay," he said. "I had received a report that you were going around town collecting money from merchants for some advertising scheme. You just have to be careful about this kind of thing." He told me a man had overheard part of a conversation I had with one of the merchants. This man thought I should be reported to the police. He called in to have me picked up—hence my sudden departure from the bank.

"You're all right. You may go, and good luck to you."

"Thank you, sir."

I shook his hand, collected my material, and turned to walk out. My mind was on that woman bank president. I wanted the last contract signed so I could head to the next college campus.

Just as I reached the door, a police lieutenant bounded into the room.

"Don't let him go. I've been on the phone with the University Athletic Department, and they want to talk to him."

"But—" The chief started to protest and vouch that I was okay, but the lieutenant proceeded to tell the chief that the athletic club at the college had published a desk pad like the one I was selling and they didn't want another one done by an "outsider."

"All right," the chief said to me. "Stay until these people get here."

In a few minutes, in strode four men. I was told that they were football coaches. They all sat down and stared at me while one of them fired questions.

Finally, the questioner said, "We want you to abandon this project."

I told them I wasn't willing to do that. I talked about free enterprise, competition, and a free country. They were not impressed.

Turning to the chief, the head coach demanded that I be run out of town.

"For what reason?" the chief queried.

The coach didn't know. They walked around wringing their hands. Finally, one of them asked, "Doesn't he need a license to sell?" Everyone rushed to the chief's desk.

"I don't think so," he said, "but let me call the city attorney."

The chief dialed and spoke at length about my enterprise. He hung up and announced to the gathering of coaches, policemen, and me that the attorney would look through the city code and call back in a few minutes.

We waited. After a long while, he called back. Yes, I needed a license. It would cost $270.00. The coaches were pleased as punch. They smiled at each other, at the chief, and at me. Then they held a conference around the chief's desk. Their decision was announced to me: be jailed for violating this license law, or leave the desk pad with them and get out of town. My decision was sad but not difficult. I thanked the chief for his attitude, turned around, and walked out. My two days in Athens were a total loss. I didn't even say goodbye to the woman bank president.

For less dramatic reasons, we were unable to publish desk pads at a couple of other colleges, but we were successful for three consecutive years in giving them out at Auburn University, Howard College, Georgia Tech, and the University of Alabama.

Another successful publishing adventure we undertook in college was the publication of a student telephone directory at the University of Alabama. Again, most of our money was made from the sale of advertising to local merchants. Additional revenue was realized from the sale of copies of the directory to students at $.25 each.

The first year we published the directory, our income from advertising and book sales were well above the cost of printing. However, we wanted to increase our profits. Our goal was to sell enough copies of the book to students to cover the printing costs so that all advertising revenues would be clear profit. To accomplish this objective, in the second year of publication we secured permission to take orders for the directory in the registration line at the beginning of fall term. We doubled the price from $.25 to $.50. A lovely high school senior I was dating along with the most beautiful girls on campus were hired to take the orders. This virtually ensured sales to all the male students. Most girls would buy them anyway. Sales of directories more than doubled, thus quadrupling income from this source. We made more than $7,000.00 in profits on the student directory that year.

What's His Name?

It was July 1958. I was seventeen, 5 feet, 10 inches tall, and it was the summer before my senior year of high school. I was interested in dating someone tall. Other girls my age wore high heels, and I desired that, too.

My parents were out for the evening attending a banquet. My sister had married the previous summer. This particular summer evening, I was home alone when the phone rang.

The caller asked, "Is this Joan?"

I responded, "No, my name is Linda."

"Do you know Joan?"

"Joan, who?" I asked.

He replied, "Joan Caldwell." I knew of Joan Caldwell, but I did not know her father's name or where she lived.

He explained how he had met this person, a ticket seller, at a movie theater when he was waiting to talk to the manager about buying an ad on a desk pad. He further explained that by the time he finished his business with the manager, Joan had left, and the manager said it was against policy to give out personal telephone numbers of his employees. So he was calling all the Caldwells in the Tuscaloosa telephone directory.

While I flipped through my directory, the caller asked if I belonged to a church.

"Yes, Alberta Baptist." He said there was someone in law school with him who attended that church.

Our conversation developed to the point that the caller forgot about looking for Joan, and I forgot what my parents had taught me about talking to strangers. I guess I figured he was an okay sort of fellow if he was a law student and knew someone who went to my church.

I asked him, "How tall are you?"

When he replied, "six-four," I nearly dropped the phone. That he was in law school and tall really interested me.

After we talked about thirty minutes, he asked if he could take me to the University Student Center for a soda. I gave him directions to my house. I didn't think he would ever remember all the turns. Amazingly, in a few minutes, I saw a car coming up our driveway.

I was back home and he was gone by the time my parents returned around 10:30 p.m. I was excited to tell Mother and Daddy about meeting this tall law student. Needless to say, they were not excited at all! They were more concerned about their daughter going out with a stranger and, on top of that, someone much older.

"What's his name?" Mother asked.

"His name? Uh . . . . Oh, no. I can't remember!"

Needless to say, that didn't help my situation.

I remembered the man would be going to my father's store the next afternoon to talk with him about buying an ad on the desk pad. I asked Daddy to be sure and get his name for me.

It was Millard Fuller.

—Linda Fuller

Chapter 19

Building on Success

Publishing the student directory gave us access to information about the students, such as birthdates and home addresses. A little research turned up the interesting information that approximately sixteen students on campus had a birthday every day. We decided to form a birthday cake service. We called it "The Bama Cake Service." At the beginning of each school year, we addressed post cards to all parents and stacked them in chronological order according to the birthdates of the students. We then systematically mailed these cards every day for all students whose birthdays were two weeks later. The parents were advised of the birthday cake service and given a list of cakes they could order for their student. To order, they simply tore off the bottom portion of the card, checked the appropriate square to indicate the cake they wanted, and mailed it to us. We picked up the cards daily at the post office and called in orders to a local bakery with which we had made a deal. In the late afternoon, the baker delivered the cakes for that day to my room. After study time, either Dees or I personally delivered them to the students in their dorm rooms or apartments.

For three years, we sold an average of four cakes per day at an average profit of $2.00 per cake.

Early in our business, Dees and I began to invest earnings from our various ventures and direct-mail profits into real estate. First, we secured a long-term lease on a dilapidated six-room house near the campus. We cleaned it up, did a bit of remodeling inside, painted it, and subleased rooms to university students. I moved into one of the front rooms to manage the house. Our rental income was about double our expenses on the property. After we leased the backyard to

Falling in Love

Millard came to my house on Saturday evening and we decided to take my portable record player to the concrete patio. As we started dancing, I remember Millard pulling me close to him. Mother and Daddy were in the house, but basically we were in our own little world. I didn't have strong feelings for him at that time but I knew enough to know that our relationship was definitely getting "hot," and I didn't know quite how to handle it.

I wondered where this was leading. I was glad he liked me so much. On the other hand, at seventeen, I wasn't ready to get so serious in a relationship.

My mother cautioned me about dating this "older" man. Being a natural-born salesman, Millard figured out how to explain away this big age difference. His line of reasoning went something like this: "Right now the difference between seventeen and twenty-three years of age seems like a lot. However, the older we get the less difference it will seem. For instance, when you are thirty and I am thirty-six, that won't seem like much. The older we get, the smaller the gap." And so it went. As I got to know him and enjoy his company, our big age difference mattered less and less. My parents grew to like him, too.

Millard was the most interesting, energetic, intelligent person I had ever met, and most of all he was 6'4"!

A few months after we started dating, Millard informed me, "You are going to marry me." None of this getting-down-on-your-knees business. He just told me that I was going to marry him! I didn't give him an answer. I didn't need to.

—Linda Fuller

owners of two house trailers, income was *more* than double our expenses.

Next, we were able to purchase a large two-story house and an adjacent four-unit apartment house at the other end of the block from our rooming house. We renovated the large house and converted it into four student apartments. Both buildings were painted inside and out. New shrubbery was planted and the yard cleaned up. Dees and I personally did most of this work at nights, on weekends, and during holidays.

Our final acquisition of real estate was a vacant lot situated between the apartment house and our rooming house. On it we placed an old army barracks building. A professional house mover was hired to move the building from its original location to the lot. It was cleaned up, renovated, painted, and converted into three student apartments. My dad came to campus for a week to help with this job.

By graduation time, we owned almost half a city block. More than forty students rented rooms, apartments, and trailer space from us, and we were collecting $800.00 a month in rent.

In our senior year, we sold these holdings at a profit of $14,000.

Letter to Cousin Donald Moore

(typed on Fuller & Dees Heart of Dixie Products letterhead)
July 1, 1959
Donald Moore
Shawmut, Alabama

Greetings from the Capstone.

Lo and behold, Moore, it mightily appeareth that your good friend, M. D. Fuller, late of the single status, is about to join the ranks of the joined up—and I don't mean with Uncle Sam. Stars and the great host on the Milky Way have lately been blurring my vision to the extent that my cerebellum has failed to function properly. As a consequence, I have entered into an agreement from which I shall not be able to extricate myself. But, I'll not bemoan my plight; rather I shall rejoice. You see, in a sense I'm caught. But, in another sense I'm set free—with a very lovely young lady. For all the possible disadvantages of the married state, with little effort, I can find twice or thrice the advantages. I'm not sad, but glad for with all considerations I am convinced that the transition which is to take place within my marital status is to open doors to finer things, is to lead to the heights of human happiness. I'll see— and I'm sure you will see too, in due course.

Enough of this. Now, down to cases. Moore, old buddy, pal, friend, comrade, I would be very honored if you would be in my wedding on 30 August at 4:00 P.M. C.S.T. as an usher. This date is on a Sunday. Linda and I planned the wedding for a Sunday so it would be more convenient for all concerned to attend. If you can be an usher, naturally, you will have to come over one day early to be in a rehearsal. I'll have an apartment for you to stay in that night and other nights if you'd like to come earlier or stay later. The wedding will be semi-formal so you'll have to have a tuxedo (with a white jacket).

Drop me a card as soon as you can on this matter. I'm counting on you.

Come to see me before that time if you can find the time. I'm always glad to have you. Take it easy. I'll see you.

'Til then,
Millard

From a financial standpoint, our real estate venture was a great success, but the business was not without problems. As anyone who has either owned rental property or lived in rented living space knows, there is almost a natural conflict between the landlord and tenant. This is caused by opposite interests. The landlord wants maximum income from his investment with minimum expenses and trouble. He doesn't want his property damaged by the renter and doesn't like spending profits to make repairs. The tenant, on the other hand, wants to pay the least rent possible but wants the unit in tip-top condition. Also, because a renter doesn't own the property, he takes no responsibility for fixing or maintaining anything. Most of the time, this conflict of interest expresses itself in mild forms. With students, the conflict often easily erupted into violent forms.

One night, I was getting ready for bed in the rooming house when I heard sirens at the other end of the block. I quickly slipped on my pants and ran down there. Police, firefighters, and a host of other people, including the university dean of men and dean of housing, were standing around our big house on the corner.

The action was over even before the fire truck arrived, but I soon learned what had caused the ruckus. The boys in one of the apartments came in earlier that evening about half drunk. First, they climbed on the roof and danced around a while. Next, they went inside to continue their wild antics. One of them found an axe. He ripped three doors off the hinges and chopped them up. This wood was then piled in the middle of the floor. They lit a fire and started dancing around it. The neighbors saw and heard them and called the fire department and university officials. When the boys heard the fire truck coming, they stomped out the fire and attempted to appear as if nothing had happened. But with shattered doors lying around, the floor smoldering, and the room filled with smoke, it was hard to cover up.

The dean of men was most upset by this occurrence. He asked that all the boys who participated in the "fun" come into his office the following day. He also asked me to come see him.

Meanwhile, I found out who did the chopping. I told him that night that we expected payment for all the damage. In addition to the destroyed doors, a large area was burned in the floor. I told the ringleader of the group that I would hold him responsible for the damage.

He did not say anything in reply. The next day, I went back and told him again that we expected payment for the damage. This time he became arrogant and said he wouldn't pay for anything.

I didn't argue with him. I just went down and took out a warrant for his arrest for maliciously destroying property. The police came and put him in jail.

This got fast results. His father was at my door early the next morning, furious at our jailing his son but ready to talk about paying for damages. Upon receiving a check for half the damages and a promise to pay the other half at an early date, we dropped the charges. At the end of the semester, the son left college, and we never collected the other half of the promised payment.

The dean of students severely reprimanded the students. He also requested that we try to keep better order in our apartment buildings. I was definitely in favor of that!

When we put the barracks building on the lot behind our apartment house, the neighbor to the rear of it got so upset that we thought she might have a stroke or heart attack and die. I understood why she did not like the idea of a barracks in her backyard. It looked terrible when we moved it there. She came to the property line for several days and screamed at us every chance she got. We tried to tell her that we would soon completely remodel the building, but she would not listen. When we tried to speak to her, she went into her house. Less than a week later, she had a block mason build a horrible-looking wall ten feet high on her back lawn. We heard nothing from her after that.

In spite of these problems, during the last year of law school, we grossed nearly $20,000 from real estate rentals in addition to the sale of the property, and more than $30,000 from our various other enterprises, sandwiching them between classes and studies.

Our Wedding Day

A few days after I graduated from Tuscaloosa High School in May 1959, Millard gave me an engagement ring. I had already enrolled for summer classes at the University of Alabama_because I wanted to live in a dorm to be closer to Millard. We decided to get married between the summer and fall terms, and the ceremony would be on Sunday afternoon, August 30.

It was challenging to begin my freshman year and plan for a wedding at the same time, but we were excited, and I was actually able to do well in my studies. In addition, Millard and Morris continued to involve me in their various money-making activities.

The most important task was addressing thousands of envelopes for a mailing to all YMCA Tri-Hi-Y (girls) and Hi-Y (boys) Clubs in the United States. With the sale of holly wreaths so successful among the local clubs, we decided to expand nationwide. This was essential for us to have money to live on. The other thousands of dollars were tied up in houses rented to students. We lived in one of the two-room rental units during Millard's last term of law school.

Millard, Morris, and I had determined that all envelopes must be addressed, stuffed, and ready to mail before our wedding date so the high school clubs would receive the holly wreath promotion at the beginning of the school year. They needed time to get organized for their holiday fundraisers. I was still addressing envelopes on Saturday before the wedding. Relatives were arriving, so we put some of them to work stuffing and placing stamps on envelopes.

On the day of the wedding, Eunice, Millard's stepmother, had brought an entire turkey and dressing meal for us to eat after church. We warmed up the food and ate in what would become our little apartment. For some reason, I had not taken into consideration making time to wash my hair and get dressed for the 4:00 p.m. wedding. Everything seemed to turn into chaos.

I went home, loaded my wedding gown into the car, and took off to the church. Much to my horror, the air conditioning had been turned off, and it was hot as blazes in the bridal room. I guess I assumed someone would be around to help me with the tiny buttons on the back of my dress. It was 3:45 when I realized that the only thing I could do was wrap the dress around myself and run from the front of the sanctuary to the stairs leading to the balcony, where I knew my dad could help me. Somehow I was able to put on my veil and pull myself together before walking down the aisle.

Following the reception, Millard and I went to my house to change clothes. I slipped into a new dress, hat, and gloves I had bought for the occasion. Meanwhile, we saw that friends were arriving and looking for our getaway car. The night before, Millard had parked it in back of a neighbor's house. In order to get to the car without anyone seeing us, we decided to jump out of the bedroom window and make a mad dash for it. Much to my horror, the netting on my hat got caught on a tree, slowing us down a bit. (We laughed about this later, remembering how funny my little hat looked dangling from that branch.)

By the time we got to the car, our "friends" had raised the hood in an attempt to keep us from driving away. Millard cranked up the car anyway and proceeded down the driveway and took off down the street. The hood was still up when we came to a stop at the first traffic light. I jumped out quickly to slam it closed. We took off as fast as we could with about ten cars blowing their horns behind us in fast pursuit. Momentarily, we gained enough distance to dart into a convenience store, swerving to miss gasoline pumps. Just as we pulled around behind the building, we were relieved to see the line of cars go zipping by. Whew! We had lost them!

Both of us were wringing wet with sweat as we started driving toward Birmingham, where we were spending a three-day honeymoon—the first night in the bridal suite of a Holiday Inn. The next day, we went into downtown Birmingham to eat at a popular cafeteria. The spike heels I wore caught on the carpet at the top of the stairs and I literally went flying. People eating downstairs heard the commotion and rose to their feet in shock. As I scrambled to stand, I could see that one of the long, skinny heels of my shoes had snapped. Luckily I had no injuries except for a few abrasions. Ruffles of what we called back then a "stiff petticoat" dragged as I hobbled into a nearby rest room.

Millard was pretty shaken from seeing his bride go sailing. Even so, he managed to find his way to a shoe store. Later we laughed about this incident, saying that it was no way to "fall in love." Even though business was booming, we were cash poor because all assets were tied up in property. This meant that a pair of shoes was not in our meager honeymoon budget.

—Linda Fuller

Chapter 20

Riding High on Tractor Cushions

I graduated from law school in January 1960 and immediately entered the Army at Fort Sill, Oklahoma, for a six-month period of active duty. I had received a second lieutenant's commission through an ROTC program at the university the previous May.

My first three months at Fort Sill were spent in Artillery School. Then I was transferred to the Judge Advocate Section, where I spent the remainder of my tour as a legal assistant officer. At night, during the last three-month period, I taught a business law course at nearby Cameron Junior College in the town of Lawton.

Journal entries:

8 April 1960
Lawton, Oklahoma
Only three weeks remain in my schooling in the Artillery and Missile School. The course, which began on 6 February, has been generally dull to me. However, there have been a few bright and interesting moments. The subjects that have interested me most are organization and tactics. Observing artillery fire is also fascinating. The whole system of placing artillery fire on a target is interesting, but I get very bored when it comes down to the details. . . . Maybe I am doing best by spending a minimum of time on the artillery work and spending as much time as possible in reading, writing, and thinking about the business back in Tuscaloosa and the prospects of the law business in August.

9 April 1960
Lawton

Linda and I spent the morning at Ft. Sill jumping from Thrift Shop to PX to Quartermaster to Thrift Shop back to Quartermaster, etc. looking for the articles of clothing for the summer uniforms. The Thrift Shop had TW browses for as cheap as $.25, but none of them fit me. Finally, I bought a TW at the QM for $14.35, which was at half price. None of the places we looked had Third Army patches, nor did they have an Overseas cap that would fit me. I guess I'll get those items Monday PM or have Linda pick them up downtown this afternoon.

I hate to spend the money for the uniforms, even though we did receive a $300 allowance. Some of the ones we buy will be worn only once in all probability. If a system could be worked out whereby we would only have to buy what we really needed to accomplish our mission while in the Army, a tremendous amount of money could be saved . . . .

13 April 1960
Lawton

. . . Last evening I attended the final rehearsal of the Easter Pageant. Linda attended a class on Russian language.

Participation in the pageant has been a real fine experience for both Linda and me. The annual event serves as a source of spiritual strength to the people of this area who take advantage of it. I wish everyone in the nation could see it.

8 May 1960
Lawton

Last week marked the end of my Artillery school; it also marked the beginning of my "career" in the Judge Advocate Section. . . . The experience I'll gain while here for the remaining three months will be valuable to me both in the private practice of law and in my career as a reserve officer.

I became one of several legal assistants. As such, I apprised military personnel of their legal rights in various matters. The experience was valuable training in the science of extracting information from a client in preparation for a lawsuit or simply to inform a person of his rights.

My first "client" on Wednesday was a former classmate of mine in the just completed Artillery course, one Lieutenant Chapman from West Virginia. He was about to depart for Korea and desired a power of attorney and a will. This was prepared for him by a sergeant in the office, Sgt. Long, after I had provided him with the facts.

Since the legal assistance officer wasn't in on Wednesday, I had to take additional phone calls. I found myself advising people over the phone who just a few days earlier had been my instructors at the school.

26 June 1960
Lawton

The day is drawing nigh when we shall depart this installation. I shall not be sad.

We have made the best of our stay here, I think, but in the whole matter there is the feeling that we are working toward nothing definite and concrete.

I am enjoying and benefiting greatly from teaching a course in Business Law at nearby Cameron College. Certainly, one learns better when he has to prepare well enough to teach a subject. In my case, I feel that I am benefiting not only from a better familiarization with the subject matter of the course, but also with the speaking experience.

In the line of speaking experience, I have been getting more than that at the college. Last week, it was my privilege and pleasure to address over 2,000 enlisted men on the subject of "Dollars and Sense." The talk was made to about 700 men at each of three sessions on Tuesday, Wednesday, and Thursday and lasted, each session, for about 50 minutes. The talks concerned a consideration of contract theory, special kinds of contracts, and the sale of equities in homes. I spiced the talks with jokes and humorous stories to keep the troops awake. This I did on the theory that no man can learn a thing if he is asleep. I kept them awake and the boys enjoyed the talks, I believe. On the last day of the talks, when I ascended the stage I was applauded. The talk was interrupted once with applause, and they applauded when I finished.

Linda is now 10 days overdue on this "having a baby" business. We are both anxious to see the little fellow. Maybe he will make a grand entrance this week. We certainly hope so.

4 July 1960
Lawton, OK
The doctor says a baby is on the way. Linda determined this morning about 7:30 that she was having labor pains. We have been waiting almost three weeks now for our "addition" to arrive, so we were indeed happy to learn that something was about to give.

It was pouring rain when we drove out to the hospital on post. After signing Linda in, I returned to the house where I am about to begin preparation for my next class at Cameron College. It is still raining. In fact, it is raining harder now than it was earlier this morning. As Linda says, "It is a good day to have a baby."

10:55 p.m.: We had a boy. He came at 4:36. Weight 8 lbs, 15 oz. Length 21 inches. Head of real black hair—a good looking fellow. We named him Christopher.

Linda did real well. Major Cochrane, who delivered the baby, said she was an excellent patient. That's my gal! She's the most wonderful woman I've ever known. I love her, love her, love her.

In August, I was released from duty, and Linda and I immediately went to Montgomery, where I rejoined Morris Dees to open our law office and continue our business operations. He had graduated from the University Law School at the same time I left the army.

In the weeks that followed, we worked diligently to establish ourselves in our new law practice, compiling a list of all lawyers in the city. Every day we visited a few of them. These contacts proved helpful because the lawyers began referring cases to us that they did not want to handle. Most of this referral work involved small matters, such as collection cases or misdemeanor criminal cases, but we were glad to get it.

The real estate firm from which I purchased a house started bringing us a few loan closings. Announcements of the opening of our office were sent to a long list of business and professional people and to friends. The local newspaper ran a story on the opening of our law office. Soon total strangers were coming into the office to employ our firm. Even before we graduated from the university, Dees and I had decided upon a division of work in the law practice. My areas of responsibility would be real estate matters, business agreements, collections, bankruptcy, and debtor's court cases. He would handle criminal cases, taxation, domestic relations, and tort cases. On unusual and difficult matters, we would collaborate. This would include all cases that went to trial. Our agreement seemed to be working out well.

29 November 1960
Montgomery, Alabama
Since the 4th of July, I've been one busy person. After getting out of the Army on 3 August, Linda and I—and Chris—returned to Tuscaloosa where I finished selling advertising for the 1960–61 student directory. We stayed with the Caldwells (Linda's parents) for about a month. During that month, I made a few trips to Montgomery to check on some business, such as finding a place to live and talking with Morris. He had recently finished law school, liquidated most of our business ventures, and was getting his family settled in the Pike Road area near Montgomery where he grew up.

Linda and I rented an apartment in the Cloverdale and Huntingdon College area and lived there only a few weeks until we purchased a house. With four bedrooms and two bathrooms, it seemed huge in comparison to the two-room apartment we lived in during my last semester of law school and the tiny three-room house during our six months in Lawton, Oklahoma.

We had very little furniture. Most had been loaned or given to us by Mr. and Mrs. Dees, Linda's parents, and others. Purchasing a couple of secondhand chairs for the den provided the basics. . . . Linda has been hard at work making curtains for the house. Tonight, we hope to put up the last ones in the parlor.

Life in the law office has been exciting but hectic. Every case is a crisis. The most perplexing part of practicing law is the uncertainty of the whole business. You never seem to know exactly whether or not your position is sound. I seem to constantly grope in the dark. We have been making no fantastic amount of money, but we seem to be meeting expenses and that, I suppose, is an accomplishment to some degree. We have several cases pending that should bring in some amount of money. Beverly, Morris's wife, is our secretary for the time being.

The holly wreath business is off some this year. I think it is due to the fact that the price increased twenty cents per wreath over last year's price. We may make more money than last year though because of a better profit margin. . . .

Something new is the test we are now running on selling tractor cushions. We mailed sample cushions to 24 Future Farmers of America leaders asking that they conduct a test sale. . . . Conducting such a large sale will cost plenty of money, so we want to be sure before we jump in deep.

. . . This afternoon, Morris and I brainstormed about ways to make money. I delight in talking about unique schemes and then in putting them into operation. Among other things, we discussed publishing a composite book of college humor. The idea would be to subscribe to all college humor magazines and take excerpts from all of them and write one large fun book to be distributed to all colleges through campus bookstores. Another was to start a birthday cake telegraph delivery service. We discussed a local business of selling seconds of name brand clothing—such as Arrow shirts. We talked about a Montgomery birthday greeting book. Another idea was a newspaper clipping service . . . .

But our best bet right now, I think, is the tractor cushions.

Law practice was always stimulating and exciting. I tried and won my first case in circuit court in January 1961. It was a simple collection case. My client loaned the defendant $770.00, and the defendant then later refused to repay it. I won the case easily, but then the defendant filed bankruptcy proceedings. We never collected a cent, but it sure felt good to win the first case.

The same day I won my first case, Dees was defending a woman in city court charged with selling alcoholic beverages on Sunday. The judge heard most of the case and then excused himself after realizing he owned the café where the defendant allegedly sold the alcoholic beverages. A new judge assumed the bench. As soon as he was seated, Dees entered a plea of double jeopardy. The judge took the plea under advisement, recessed the hearing, and a few days later held in favor of our client, deciding that, indeed, she had been in "jeopardy." The case was dismissed.

The most dramatic incident in our young law firm involved a divorce proceeding. Dees was representing a young woman in the case. She told him her husband would not contest the divorce. Papers were drawn up accordingly, and the husband was asked to come in and sign. I happened to be in Dees's office when the man arrived. I noticed that he was tense and nervous. I walked into my office, but I heard the conversation through the door.

"I don't like this," the man said. "I don't want a divorce. I don't want to lose my wife and family. I can't go through with this."

He repeated this over and over.

Finally, he said, "I'm going out of here and shoot myself."

"You don't have to go out," Dees replied. "I have a gun in my desk. You can just shoot yourself here."

Dees opened his drawer and handed the man a .38 pistol.

The man pushed his chair back, stood up, closed his eyes, put the gun to his head, and pulled the trigger.

"Click." The gun was empty.

The man slumped to his chair, perspiring profusely.

There was a long, long silence. Then he extended his hand across the desk.

"Thanks for saving my life." He got up and left without signing the papers. As far as I know, he was reconciled to his wife, and they stayed together.

We worked diligently on every case that came to us, no matter how small or seemingly insignificant. No client of ours ever felt that we were neglecting his or her case. We soon got a reputation for hard work. Former clients referred their friends to us. Our law practice grew steadily from the day we started until we retired from the active practice of law to devote full time to our rapidly growing business a year and a half later.

Meanwhile, we continued our business operations. Many of our enterprises at college—the cake service, student telephone directory, desk pads, etc.—came to an end because they were strictly campus activities, but our direct-mail business of selling holly wreaths and door mats to groups for fundraising continued. We also began to seek other products for this phase of our business.

Early in October I met Hilliard Aronov, president of Fabrics, Inc., in Montgomery. He and I started out talking about selling rag dolls that he manufactured and ended up talking about tractor cushions.

As soon as he mentioned the tractor cushions, I remembered that Dees was active as a high school student in the Future Farmers of America. In fact, he had told me about being the "Star Farmer of Alabama" one year.

What could possibly be a more natural fundraising item for the FFA than tractor cushions? I thought.

Mr. Aronov took me back into his plant and showed me some of the cushions. They were beautiful. I was becoming more excited by the minute. After getting approximate cost figures on the cushions, I tore back to the office to share this new idea with Dees.

When I walked in, he was sitting behind his desk.

"Tractor cushions," I said slowly.

He looked puzzled.

"FFA."

Like a bolt of lightning, he shot up out of his desk and banged a closed fist against his palm.

"It'll work!" he exclaimed.

That's all it took to communicate an idea. Three words and we were on the same page. This is a classic example of why we worked so well together.

We were both sure the idea of selling tractor cushions to the FFA would work, but for "insurance," we wanted more definite proof. Immediately, we started working on a small test mailing to randomly selected FFA chapters throughout the country. Orders came in from this mailing better than expected. By December we were making plans for a nationwide promotion to all Future Farmers of America chapters in the United States.

The Ford Motor Company was contacted and arrangements made to purchase at cost a Ford tractor to offer as the top prize in a nationwide tractor cushion sales contest. In January, we dropped 10,000 tractor cushions in the mail to the FFA chapter advisors. A separate letter told them about the new project, the top prize of a Ford tractor, and how to order.

Within two weeks, we were flooded with orders from all over the country.

On February 18, 1961, I recorded in my diary, "Our business continues to grow. The tractor cushion sale is booming. As of today, we have almost 1,000 customers. . . . We really have a good deal going and I'm firmly convinced that we are going to make at least $50,000 net profit on the venture and may well net $75,000. We shall see."

On March 12, I again recorded in the diary, "The tractor cushion sale is progressing nicely. We counted last night that almost 22,000 cushions have been shipped by Fabrics and our total orders—including those not yet shipped—are around 38,000. We have had to turn down over 300 customers so far because Mr. Aronov is not sure he can meet the demand of more customers. We now are over the 1100 mark on customers."

This tremendous burst of business brought us a critical cash-flow problem. We had understood at the beginning of the project that Mr. Aronov would extend credit until collections started coming in from our customers. A few days after the sale started, however, he informed us that he could extend no more than $20,000. We were desperate. Orders were pouring in, and we didn't have an extra source of money to meet this unexpected need. Mr. Aronov threatened to withhold further shipments to our customers unless we kept the account paid down to a $20,000 balance.

Reflections

Up over the horizon, I see dimly a light shining for me— leading, beckoning me to it. But the road to the light is rugged and rough, the obstacles are many and seemingly insurmountable. The going looks rough indeed. But alas, the huge surge inside me pushes me on. I try to go and I fall back. Downhearted, I feel that the whole of God's universe is against me. The worth of anything quizzes me. These problems are terrible because my mind circles and whizzes and buzzes. And, even though I wonder what the light holds for me, is it worth the effort? Do I really want it? How do I know? There I go, wondering.

—Millard Fuller (1958)

Mr. Aronov called a meeting for the purpose of discussing the crisis. When we arrived for the meeting, an unexpected group of men was in the room. Mr. Aronov got down to business. These men wanted to buy a 50 percent interest in our company. They would keep the balance paid down to the $20,000 limit. We would be freed to concentrate on handling details of the promotion.

"Not interested. Not at all interested," we told them. We wouldn't even discuss price. This was our deal, and we would run it somehow or watch it go under. In no case would we sell a percentage to anyone.

Our resolve was so firm that the matter of purchase was dropped within minutes. Next, we turned to talking about how Mr. Aronov could extend us more credit. After a long discussion and an agreement to draw up a certain assignment of accounts, he said he would extend our line of credit up to $60,000. This was not enough to meet the forthcoming need, but it was a step in the right direction.

We went to one of the local banks seeking a loan. They turned us down saying that the deal was not sound because we didn't have signed contracts from our customers. Next, we went back to Tuscaloosa to the First National Bank, where we had banked while running our business in college. They loaned us $25,000. Still not enough. I went to my dad. He mortgaged his house and farm in order to lend us money. He co-signed on a note at the National Bank in Opelika, Alabama, where we borrowed $10,000. An aunt of mine loaned us $500. Dees's father signed a note so we could get more money. By the "skin of our teeth," we came through the crisis. By late March, collections began to come in and the pressure eased off.

As our business continued to grow in future years, we faced other financial problems but none like the one related to tractor cushions. It was a happy day when we repaid all the loans that summer. When the sale finally ended in May, we tallied our results: 65,000 cushions shipped! It was hard to visualize, so we estimated that number to represent 20 rail cars packed full. Orders were received for nearly 100,000, but even with Aronov's plant working around the clock, Mr. Aronov could not keep up. We had to refuse orders for 30,000 cushions. The sale was a success beyond our wildest dreams.

An FFA chapter in Willow Hill, Pennsylvania, won the Ford tractor. Dees drove up there in June to present it to them.

The following year, we secured five Ford tractors as prizes, plus rifles for lesser awards. The initial glamour of the project for the FFA chapters had worn off by then, and our total sales were less than the previous year, but we still sold thousands of cushions. Before the tractor cushion project finally ended, we made more than $50,000 profit from the idea.

During this initial phase of our business in Montgomery, we operated our law office and business enterprises out of a rented suite of offices consisting of three small rooms. One room was my office, one was Dees's office, and the other served as a reception area. We started out with one employee in the reception room. As the tempo of business increased, we added another person, then another and another. When the reception area was full of desks, we crammed others into our tiny offices. When there was absolutely no more room, women were hired to come at night to type letters and process orders. Still others were hired to type at home. Dees and I worked day and night to keep up with everything.

In early May, we took part of the money we made from the tractor cushion sale and purchased an old two-story building in downtown Montgomery. After spending an additional $8,000 for remodeling, we moved our whole operation into our own building in early fall. We now had seven large rooms. We felt this would be adequate space for a long time. But less than six months later, we were adding a large area to the back of the building to accommodate an ever-growing work force.

Chapter 21

Pushing the Envelope

During summer 1961, we busily planned for a host of new promotions in the fall. Stadium cushions, manufactured by Fabrics, Inc., were to be tested in 400 high schools as a fundraising item. Another product we planned to test for fundraising was SPRING, a household detergent. We thought Home Demonstration Clubs might be interested in this product. We planned to offer polyester foam to Future Homemakers of America chapters and Home Demonstration Clubs.

We made plans to publish our biggest catalog of products ever for Junior Achievement companies. In it, we would offer holly wreaths, three lines of door mats, sponges, dishcloths, coat hanger covers, a stick for picking up trash, garbage can holders, and painted pinecones.

We contacted a rat poison manufacturer in Wisconsin and made arrangements to offer Ferret Rat Poison to FFA chapters for fundraising along with the tractor cushions.

All of these projects were undertaken in the fall. Most failed completely. Others, such as the rat poison and sponges, enjoyed moderate success and profitability, but none of them were spectacular.

One new project born during this time did succeed tremendously. Earlier that year, Dees and I had one of our frequent talk-a-thons. He picked up a *Life* magazine and started flipping through it. Suddenly, he stopped turning.

"Look," he said. I leaned over. He indicated a picture of a man pointing to a huge pile of mail stacked on the floor in front of him.

"We've got to have mail coming in here like that," Dees enthusiastically announced.

"I'm in favor," I responded.

Then our conversation grew urgent. "How can we get piles of orders pouring in here on a regular basis?"

We had experienced the exhilarating feeling of hundreds of letters pouring in with tractor cushion orders. Now, though, we didn't want hundreds. We wanted thousands! And we wanted them on a sustained basis.

Through the sale of tractor cushions to the FFA, we had learned the importance of finding a product that "fits" the organization. We decided we needed to find another deal for some other organization. We needed the right product to offer them.

Finally, one of us said, "What about Future Homemakers of America?"

"Yes, that's a big nationwide youth organization. What can we sell through them for fundraising?"

We already planned to test polyester foam with FHA, but neither of us was excited about it. We needed something more natural—more logical—for them.

For hours that day we scratched our heads over this problem. We knew the Future Homemakers were just as numerous as the FFA. With the right product for them, we could stack up the orders.

But we couldn't think of an idea. We met several more times in the next few days without results.

Then, one day a few weeks later, Dees walked into my office and quietly announced that he thought he had the right product for the Future Homemakers. He said it was a large part of our dream about the huge stacks of mail.

"What is it?" I asked.

"A cookbook."

"That's it!"

It was my turn to jump up and bang a fist against my palm. Dees had just been to the state office of Vocational Home Economics seeking addresses of local Future Homemakers chapters so he could send out the mailing of the polyester foam. By accident, he saw in the office of the state director a small cookbook that was published for state chapters. He asked a few questions and found that the book was selling at a fantastic rate and that no other state in the nation was publishing a cookbook for their chapters. Dees immediately realized the possibilities. He rushed to the office to hear my reaction.

We obtained a list of every home economics teacher in the nation. A letter went out appealing for favorite meat recipes. Some teachers were so excited about having their recipe and name in a book that they sometimes sent more than one. We compiled the recipes and organized them into categories, sprinkling photos among them and adding a table of contents and index. By January, this first cookbook was ready.

Promotions on the book went out to eleven thousand chapters. We did not wait long. Within a week, orders began flooding in. The response totally eclipsed the best days of the tractor cushion sales. We sold cookbooks by the tens of thousands, and the orders increased by leaps and bounds.

On January 22, I wrote in my diary, "The cookbook, *Favorite Recipes of American Home Economics Teachers*, is off the press! First copies were mailed to home economics teachers last week. Three days ago, our first orders came back. First day, one thousand books sold. Second day, eighteen hundred books sold. Third day, twenty-two hundred books sold. I am sure that the next batch of mail will bring forth three thousand to five thousand in book sales."

After this book succeeded so well, we began to publish cookbooks for other organizations. Within two years, we were the largest publisher of cookbooks in the country . . . if not the world!

In the meantime, we continued to add new products and publish other books. A series of Junior Achievement Yearbooks and a Directory of High School Coaches were started in 1962. The J.A. Yearbook was simply a printing venture. Certain sections of the books were standardized for all yearbooks in the country. Other sections were different for each city. We supplied kits for putting the books together. Local J.A. areas supplied us with materials for their city. We contracted with a printing company to print the designated number of yearbooks for each locality, with their local material incorporated with the standard sections.

The Directory of High School Coaches was, in effect, an almanac for high school coaches. It listed all coaches in the United States and indicated the sports they coached. It also gave many statistics about state and regional championships, field dimensions, track records, etc., of interest to those in the coaching profession. The books were mailed free of charge to all high schools in the country. We made money from the sale of advertisements to sporting goods manufacturers.

In spring 1963, we started testing the sale of toothbrushes for fundraising. This project got off to a slow start, but within a year we were selling eighty thousand a month—an average of one million a year.

Several months before we offered toothbrushes, we had incorporated a separate company through which we offered our "manufactured" products to clubs for fundraising. This company was called "The Fuller Company." (Another company was formed for selling cookbooks—"Favorite Recipes Press"). The name "Fuller Company" brought us into conflict with the Fuller Brush Company as soon as we got into volume sales of toothbrushes. Their legal department wrote asking us to change the name of our company due to this conflict. We didn't want to change it for several reasons. After an exchange of a few letters, I flew to Hartford, Connecticut, for a conference with company officials. We agreed to add, "Not a product of the Fuller Brush Company," on all our toothbrush packages. That settled the problem for a few months. Then the legal department wrote again, this time to ask us to drop the phrase, "Not a product of the Fuller Brush Company." Again they requested that we change the name. In answer, we stated our intentions to keep it. That ended the matter. All the while, toothbrush orders increased, along with orders for most of our other products.

In spring 1963, we began to realize that we were fast growing beyond the capacities of the expanded facilities in our downtown building. For the second time, we added a night shift and hired people to work at home. The search was on again for a larger building. We found it in May—a large modern office building on the edge of town, formerly the home office of the Atlantic National Life Insurance Company. The property included two acres of beautifully wooded land. We bought it at $100,000, paying in cash.

We quickly found a tenant for our downtown building and moved to the new facility during the first week of June. Dees and I were proud of that building. On top of it was a large opaque glass panel that lit up at night. We had the "Atlantic National Life Insurance Company" lettering removed and replaced it with, "Fuller and Dees, Inc." Every time I walked in or out of the building for the first few weeks, I gazed at that sign. Other people saw it too because our phone rang regularly from friends and associates to congratulate us on the new building.

We couldn't spend too much time looking at our new sign, though, because we had planned a whole new batch of projects for the fall. There was much to do.

Twenty-two new cookbooks were planned for publication. One hundred thousand sample toothbrush packs were being readied to mail out to prospective customers. Advertising for the second edition of the National Directory of High School Coaches had to be sold. A new guidance publication for high school students about to enter college required planning.

We were particularly excited about this last project. The magazine, to be called *Off to College,* would include articles (generated from college orientation materials) such as "Why Freshmen Fail"; "How to Study"; "Should I Join a Fraternity or Sorority?"; "Campus Etiquette"; etc. A large section would contain advice on what kind of clothing and accessories to take to college. To learn what items were in vogue on campuses around the country, we hired Eugene Gilbert of New York, a foremost authority in the youth market, to conduct a survey on college campuses in every section of the United States. We would include information from this survey in the magazine. To finance the publication, we intended to sell advertising to the companies whose products were popular on college campuses. Distribution of the book was free to the one million-plus high school seniors planning to enter college in the fall.

We spent days and weeks working out the problems and details. An elaborate direct-mail campaign was planned for all prospective advertisers. Mr. Gilbert flew to Montgomery and spent three days with us making plans. After one day of work in the office, we rented a private plane and flew to Panama City, Florida, where we continued our work on the beach. We set up tables for our work right on the water's edge under large umbrellas.

As a last step in the campaign, our overall strategy included a personal call to the advertising agencies of the top prospects. In mid-September, I flew to New York and spent the next three months personally contacting the companies and agencies. The *New York Times* ran a story on the new magazine and reported my presence in the city in connection with it. I talked to dozens of advertising people both in agencies and in companies. A professional advertising sales-man was hired to help make the calls to agencies. By Christmas, we had commitments for more than $50,000 in advertising, but that was not enough. We needed three times that amount to break even. After long weeks of agonizing, we admitted defeat on the project. More than $40,000 was spent on advertising promotions, not including executive time, and we still failed.

Someone once said, "The mark of a good executive is his ability to distinguish between the difficult and the impossible." On this occasion, we were poor executives because I am sure what we under-took was impossible as we had conceived it—free distribution to all high school students planning to attend college, to be financed by the sale of advertising.

The only thing that kept my New York trip from being a total failure was the sale of advertising for the Directory of High School Coaches.

We did not abandon our plans to publish *Off to College*; we merely changed our method of distribution. Instead of a free distribution financed by advertising, we decided to print in quantity and sell to high schools at a low price. This proved to be a feasible plan, for we sold nearly two hundred thousand copies the first year, and volume increased in ensuing years.

The failure of our plan for advertising in *Off to College* was a setback for our company, but all other projects worked even better than expected. Our company moved forward at an incredible rate of growth.

By late 1963, we were sending a panel truck to the post office to pick up mail. The picture in *Life* magazine could have been taken in our office at that point. We had turned a dream into reality in two years.

When we tallied our sales at the end of 1963, they totaled more than a million dollars! We considered this a milestone in our business, for we had dreamed of this day for a long time. In April, I had written in our diary, "My prediction is that toothbrushes will be the gimmick by which our sales will exceed one million dollars in 1963. I am hereby dedicating myself to this magic million. We're going to make it!"

On January 1, 1964, I wrote about this achievement and made another prediction: "Sales for the year exceeded one million dollars! This was a goal we had set long ago and we finally made it. Now we want ten million! We'll make it within six years, with a little luck. I look forward to 1964 with great expectation. It should be a banner year in many respects."

1964 was, indeed, a banner year in our business. We started more new projects, and the existing ones continued to grow. On February 7, I wrote, "Business is getting better and better." Again, on February 23, I noted, "Business continues to pick up. Last week we had our best week ever on toothbrush sales. Without Saturday's mail (George Washington's Birthday), the sales totaled almost 30,000 packages of brushes. We expect this total to be exceeded in the weeks ahead. Cookbook sales are holding up well. We've averaged about 30,000 sales a week for the last four weeks."

From High Heels to High Living

I was nineteen when our first child was born, and even though I was a happy mother, I wanted to complete my college education.

Millard encouraged me. He said, "We can afford tuition and a fulltime baby sitter."

Four years later, during my last year of college, I drove to school in a brand new Lincoln Continental, and Millard had, by that time, set up my own bank account, which he maintained at a minimum balance of $1,000. I went shopping for clothes and shoes every chance I got. The sky was the limit. The double closet in our bedroom became too small, so I moved Millard's clothes into another bedroom.

With me in school and Millard working twelve to fourteen hours a day, we had little time for each other except at dinner in the evenings. Often Morris ate with us since he lived in the country and it took too long for him to go home and come back. They did their business brainstorming during meals as the children and I sat and listened. Then it was a quick kiss on the cheek and back to the office.

One evening I remember making a strong attempt at keeping Millard home. As he walked out to the car, I bolted through the front door and pulled on his arm, begging him to stay home. Much to my shock and dismay, he pulled free and left anyway, saying he had to go.

I finally realized that Millard was more married to his business than he was to me and how estranged we had become.

I had once thought that a college education and a tall, rich husband would bring total contentment and happiness. Now that I had acquired all that, I could not understand why I felt so empty and distraught. Millard and I slept in the same bed, but as a matter of fact, it was as if we were worlds apart.

—Linda Fuller

On June 14, I scribbled in my diary, "Sales on the Illinois and Deep South cookbooks have been above expectations. To our surprise, sales are holding up well this summer." In July, I wrote, "Things at the office are tumbling along," and in October, "Business has never been better. From August 15 to October 15, 1963, we sold approximately

$146,000 worth of products. For the same period this year our sales were $504,000. All sales have been as good as or better than expected."

Within six months after purchasing our new building, we were talking about the need to expand it. By February 1964, final plans were drawn for a 10,000-foot addition. The enlarged building was designed to accommodate seventy-three people. It was completed in June. We moved in on the 20th and four months later, on October 25, I noted in my diary, "Employment at the office continues to increase. I believe we now have in excess of one hundred full-time people working three shifts. About a month ago we started a third shift in the typesetting department and last week we added the second shift on the Burroughs machines. We already had a second shift in our promotional, printing, and typesetting departments."

By any measure, our business was a success at the time I received Jim Waery's letter on July 30 inviting me to go overseas and witness missionary work. Sales were above expectations and profits high. Our growth was so rapid that we had difficulty adding space fast enough to accommodate new employees. Prospects were bright for even greater growth and higher sales.

I was deeply involved in every phase of the business. We were working on at least a dozen new projects, including the sale of candy for fundraising to various groups and organizations. We had only been in our newly expanded building for six weeks. Many new employees were joining the company. Most important, I felt that we were standing on the threshold of tremendous profits.

I couldn't afford to leave all this to visit missionaries! Surely anyone in his right mind would agree that I had many legitimate reasons not to accept Jim Waery's offer.

Deep inside, I knew I should go. I felt the invitation was a call from God to perform a particular service for his church. But I turned it down. In my reply to Mr. Waery, I wrote, "I'll do it in two years, maybe."

1957—The Fuller family
Back: Render, Eunice (step-mother), Millard;
Front: Nick and Doyle (youngest)

1959—Eunice, Render, Nick
and Doyle Fuller (Millard's
two half brothers).

1958—Millard Fuller and Morris Dees' first office
for "Heart of Dixie Products" located near
University of Alabama campus in Tuscaloosa.

1958—Law Day at University of Alabama
Left: Leigh Harrison, Dean of the Law School. Millard shaking hands
with Mrs. Frank Rose (wife of University of Alabama president.)

1958—Linda and Millard dressed up for ROTC Ball.

August 30, 1959—Millard and Linda say wedding vows at Alberta Baptist Church in Tuscaloosa, Alabama.

April 1960—Linda and Millard expecting first baby in Lawton, OK.

May 1960—Millard preparing to teach his Business Law class at Cameron College in Lawton, OK.

August 30, 1959—Happily exiting the church.

Millard Dean Fuller
1960 University of Alabama Law Graduate

1960—Linda, Millard and Chris (6 mos.)

1961—Render Fuller with all of his sons
and first grandson.

1962—Millard and Linda with
second baby, Kim (3 mos.)

1962—Millard, Linda, Render and Eunice
and Chris (2 yrs.)

1963—Business partners,
Millard Fuller and Morris Dees.

1963—Linda with Chris and Kim.

1964—Millard's entire immediate family.

1964—Millard keynotes at Junior Achievement
National Convention held in Cleveland.

1964—Millard, the successful
business man.

Part 3

Paradigm Shifts

(1960–1965)

Chapter 22

Thinking Twice

God sometimes calls us into service at the most inopportune times. Often we find a hundred reasons to say no.

One day, Jesus asked a couple of men to follow him. "Sir," one of them replied, "first let me go and bury my father." The other man said, "First, let me go and say goodbye to my family." Jesus answered the first man, "Let the dead bury their own dead. You go and preach the kingdom of God." He told the second man," Anyone who starts to plow and then keeps looking back is of no use for the kingdom of God" (Luke 9:59-62).

God wants our availability. He wants our hearts and minds and lives. He wants us to say in the words of Isaiah, "Here am I. Send me" (Isa 6:8).

When I was in law school, I had promised God that I would make myself available for his purposes. I had assured God that, regardless of the success or financial achievements of our company, I would always put his kingdom first.

But in a real-life situation, I said no to God and yes to business and further financial achievements.

The success of our business kept growing. A pinnacle was reached a few weeks after I read and turned down Jim Waery's invitation to go to Africa: Marilyn Black walked in with the million-dollar financial statement. A tingling sensation rushed through my entire body that day. I remained quiet and composed on the outside, but inside I bubbled. This was a goal long worked for, a dream beyond the "American Dream," a dream come true!

I had thought about and had written about this magic million dollars for years. Back at the university, I was in church one Sunday with the girl who later became my wife. I scribbled on a little pocket note pad, "A man becomes what he thinks about." I handed it to her. She looked puzzled. I then wrote a question: "Do you know what I am thinking about?" She shook her head. "One million dollars," I wrote. Years later when we remembered this incident, she told me that it seemed odd to her that rather than listening to the preacher's sermon, I was having such thoughts. She was right.

I wrote about this one million in my diary, too. In fact, I accurately predicted the year of this achievement. On May 22, 1961, I recorded, "Morris and I are discussing the possibility of going out of law practice. I think that if we do, it will be one of the wisest money moves of our lives. I think we can make a million dollars inside of three years if we concentrate our efforts on our business. We have several ideas that should pay off handsomely for us next year." Again, in January 1962, I predicted that our cookbook project was going to accomplish this objective for us: "I predict that the book will be a success for the years to come and that it will make the original 'Fuller and Dees' an outfit of joint millionaires."

We were a success not only financially. The community was heaping accolades on us. People stood in awe at the two boys just out of college who had moved from a little rented office to a large building, expanded it, bought a larger building, and then doubled its size—all in less than four years. Most people didn't know what we were doing. They did not understand our business, but they knew it was growing at a fantastic rate. Feature stories and pictures appeared in the newspapers about us and our growing business.

As I experienced inner conflicts on the occasions of receiving Mr. Waery's letter and of learning about my financial achievement from Marilyn Black, the words of praise from the community rang in my ears. "You've got it made," these voices said. "Many people would like to be in your shoes." The other voice I heard was much quieter, but nonetheless bothersome: "Where are you headed? What does all this mean? You're *not* putting God first."

Do we not all hear two voices when faced with any ethical, moral, or religious decision? Call these voices God and the devil. Call them the forces of good and evil. Call them what you will, but they're present, and you heed one of them and try to dismiss the other from your mind. I listened to the loud and "sensible" voice that said, "Man, you've got it made." The still, small voice told me I was wrong, but I had too much to lose to decide otherwise.

I remembered my promise to work hard to succeed in business and make lots of money, but that regardless of success and money, I would always seek the kingdom of God *first* in my life and share my good fortune with others. Indeed, I had kept half of the covenant—the half about success and money! God got pushed out of first place in my life long before Jim Waery wrote to me and long before Marilyn Black told me I was worth a million dollars. In fact, I started violating the covenant almost as soon as I made it.

Back at the university, I had neglected my spiritual life. There was no Congregational or United Church in Tuscaloosa. I was involved in law school and our many business activities. *Why get involved with another church?* I thought. I had no theological grounds for not joining and working in a church of another denomination. It is my belief that a person can worship God and serve in almost any church, so that was not my reason for remaining outside the church. Still, it was a good "excuse" for avoiding it.

From time to time, I attended various churches, but I was careful not to get deeply involved. If, after attending a particular church for a few weeks, I felt someone was about to ask me to assume a job there, I either started attending another church or just quit going anywhere for a while. I did not want to face a situation where I would say "no" to a request to serve in the church.

How often this happens! We do not like a confrontation. Our churches teach us to help when help is needed, not only in the church but anywhere. In the parable of the Good Samaritan, for instance, we are taught that the Samaritan is the "good guy" and those who walked on the other side of the road are the "bad guys." Who wants to be a bad guy? We simply stay alert to the needs around us and make sure we don't go near them. Who, then, can say we "walked on the other side"? We reason that if we don't directly encounter the need, then we haven't exactly ignored it.

After graduation from law school, while on active duty with the army at Fort Sill, Oklahoma, I had renewed my activity in church. A Congregational church was in nearby Lawton, Oklahoma. On the second Sunday at Fort Sill, my wife, Linda, and I joined this church. Before the six-month tour of duty ended, I had joined the choir, preached in the church, become president of the young adult Sunday school class and played a part in the annual Easter pageant at the Wichita Wildlife Refuge.

Now that I was returning to my home state of Alabama, I felt compelled to renew my close church association. It was 1956 when I left Auburn along with heavy involvements in church work and moved to Tuscaloosa to attend law school. Now it was 1960 and we were settling back in Alabama, this time in Montgomery.

Chapter 23

God or Money?

During our first six months in Montgomery, we visited various churches. To my knowledge, there was no Congregational or United Church of Christ. I later found out about First Congregational Church, attended by Negroes.

In early 1961, I learned that Harold Henderson, an old friend of mine from Pilgrim Fellowship days, had to come to Tallassee, Alabama, a town about 30 miles east of Montgomery, to assume the pastorate of a Congregational church there. I phoned and invited him to visit me at his convenience. A few days later he came with Freddy Powell, a leading church layman from Tallassee.

They had an idea. Harold and Freddy wanted me to organize a United Church in Montgomery. Actually, I had thought of such a possibility, but I intended to wait until much later to do it. These men wanted me to do it now!

An attempt had been made to start a church three years earlier. That effort had produced a list of prospects. Harold and Freddy were strong advocates of their idea and agreed to help. For these reasons, I said I would try.

In days following, all the people on their list of prospects were contacted, plus others we knew about. On Saturday night, February 11, 1961, about a dozen people gathered in our living room to organize a church. Two Sundays later we had our first Sunday school.

Starting a new church was exciting. I got caught up in the spirit of it and poured myself into it for many months. Until we secured an interim minister in late fall, I did most of the speaking in our worship services. Actually, there were a couple of interim preachers while the pulpit committee did their search. Even after getting a minister, I continued to speak occasionally.

I entered in my diary on June 2, 1962, "The pulpit committee was able to convince Harold Henderson to be the minister of our new church. I had to prepare a sermon to welcome him and his family. I plan to speak tomorrow along the general lines of the importance of what a person thinks about from day to day and what the implications are when the wrong thinking occurs in the mind from day to day."

Soon after Harold Henderson came to the church, we received approval from the Board for Homeland Ministries to proceed with the purchase of the seven acres of land for a building site. The board designated me as the attorney to handle the transaction. A title abstract on the property was secured. I read it to determine whether the owners—the Federation of Garden Clubs of Montgomery—could give us a good and clera title. To my dismay, I discovered a flaw. It was reported to the legal department of Homeland Ministries. They advised not to conclude the purchase until this defect was cleared up. What everyone thought was going to be a routine transaction quickly developed into a full-scale legal battle.

When the defect was first discovered, I brought it to the attention of the lawyer for the Federation. He and I agreed that it could be cleared if all present owners of the original tract of land that included the seven acres signed certain waivers.

The proper documents were prepared, and Reverend Henderson was given the task of getting them signed. He ran into a stone wall. Only two owners out of seven agreed to sign. The others had already heard about plans for the church to purchase the land and build there. Rumors were rampant in the neighborhood that we were going to build an "integrated" church on the property. They were pleased that we needed their consent to conclude the purchase, and they refused to sign. They did not want the church in their neighborhood.

Our only alternative was to file a suit in Equity Court to clear title to the property. To do this, the Federation lawyer and I approached the law firm that had handled the sale of the property to the Federation some years earlier. We asked that their firm file the suit and bear the expense of the litigation since they had not discovered the defect in their search of the title at the time of the earlier sale. They objected to being brought into the matter because they felt no error was made in approving the title. Conflict quickly developed among the lawyers over this difference in legal opinion.

One day, I went with the Federation lawyer to visit this law firm. We sat around a conference table and soon got into a shouting session. I accused one of the lawyers of lying about certain phases of the transaction. He jumped up and angrily demanded that I get out of his office. I refused to leave. Then he rushed out of the room, his law partner in hot pursuit. "Wait a minute," his partner urgently intoned. The door slammed shut. We could hear the muffled sounds of their voices through the door. After a few minutes, both men returned to the room. "Can't we work this thing out peacefully?" the partner asked. I nodded agreeably. I apologized for my harsh words and accusations. They agreed to file the suit, and we settled down to work out details.

When the landowners in the area were notified of the filing of the suit in court, they banded together and hired a lawyer to defend their interests. All sides prepared.

In June 1963, more than a year after the agreement was signed to purchase the property, the case went to trial. After a full hearing on the facts, the judge ruled in favor of the church and decreed that the Federation could deed us the property.

Two and a half years after holding our first Sunday school in our living room, we were ready to build a permanent "home" for our congregation. Eight months later—in February 1964—we held a groundbreaking service for our first building. It was like a regular house with most of the inside partitions left out. This large open area would be used as the worship area, or sanctuary, of the church. The completed portion of the house would be used as classrooms for our Sunday school. Later, after building the first unit of the church building, this house could either be completed and sold or used as a parsonage for the preacher and his family. The "house church" was completed, and we held the first worship service there in mid-May.

My involvement continued with the local church in the months ahead, but I also became active in the conference again. In April, I attended the annual meeting of the Southeast Convention of Congregational Churches (and acting Conference of the United Church of Christ) in Chattanooga, Tennessee. There I was elected president of the churchmen's fellowship for the entire conference. (In the same church eleven years earlier, I was elected president of the Pilgrim Fellowship.)

The burning issue at the Chattanooga conference was "realignment." The Congregational Christian Church and the Evangelical and Reformed Church had merged in 1957 to form the United Church of Christ. In following years, the former conferences of the two separate denominations were merged throughout the country. By 1964, practically every conference in the United States had merged except those in the Southeastern states. Realignment in our conference would have been simple except for the fact that within the Congregational Christian Church of the South, separate conferences existed for white and Negro churches. No one in our conference objected strenuously to the merger with the Evangelical and Reformed Churches (there were only two or three, and they were white), but many had strong objections to bringing in the twenty-five or so Negro Congregational Christian Churches.

At the 1964 meeting, the superintendent brought the matter of realignment to the floor for a vote. Advance notice had gone out from the conference office that this issue was up for vote. When the first session convened on Saturday, the church was packed from wall to wall. There was standing room only. I had never seen so many people in attendance at a church conference!

About noon, the issue of realignment was brought up for discussion. Several speakers heatedly made their points for or against the proposal. One man tried to interject the idea of communist influence in the proposal. A vote was taken, and realignment was narrowly defeated. Most rural laymen voted against the proposal. Most laymen from the larger city churches voted for it. The overwhelming majority of the preachers voted in favor.

As soon as the vote was taken, at least half of the delegates got up and walked out. These were the people who had come to defeat the proposal. They accomplished their task and left, uninterested in other phases of the conference. On the following day, I moved that realignment be put on the agenda for next year. Since most opponents of the measure had left, the motion carried.

During the ensuing year, I published a monthly newsletter in which I argued for the cause of realignment. This newsletter was mailed to all churches in the conference.

The 1965 conference was held in Atlanta, Georgia. Once again, the church was packed with delegates. We discussed and argued realignment. We voted. This time, though, the proposal carried by a slim margin. I was happy about this vote. (My joy multiplied when I saw my dad, there as a delegate from the Lanett church, standing to be counted with those voting *for* realignment.) I was glad I could play a part in giving birth to the conference that completed the realignment process of the United Church of Christ. Negro and white Congregational Christian Churches and the Evangelical and Reformed Churches united to become the Southeast Conference of the United Church of Christ. I felt this historic day in the life of our churches in the South was a victory for the kingdom of God. My role was small compared to the work done by Dr. James Lightborne, Jr., the conference superintendent, and many others. But I'll always be grateful for the opportunity of participating in this historic event.

At this conference, I was reelected president of the Churchmen's Fellowship and also elected as one of three delegates to attend the General Synod of the United Church of Christ to be held in Chicago three months later.

Without question, I was engaged in this work locally, regionally, and nationally. Friends spoke in glowing terms about my church work, especially people in my home church in Lanett. They praised me for starting the new church in Montgomery. On visits back to the church, I heard repeated exclamations like, "Oh, Millard, we are *so* proud of you! What you are doing in Montgomery with the church is wonderful! Keep up the good work." (Of course, some people became displeased with my "integration" activities and ideas. One Sunday I spoke in a church near Lanett. A longtime friend came forward after the service to greet me. "Good sermon," he said, "until you started talking about the niggers." To many white people, especially in the South, Christianity and Negroes did not mix.)

Actually, I suppose I did spend more time working for the church than many church members do. But God does not judge us by a set standard of performance. He makes a total claim on our lives and expects full use of all our talents. He judges us in terms of what we are capable of doing.

Even though I was a leader in my local church and in the conference, I gave only crumbs of my time to the work. If anything in the business conflicted with church-related activities, the business came first. I wanted to serve God through the church, but I wanted to do it at my convenience and without interfering with anything else I wanted to do.

I was happy when the church called Harold Henderson as pastor. I thought he would relieve me of much of the work with our local congregation. That was not the case, however. He wanted me to get busier than ever—making calls on prospective members, helping conclude the property sale as rapidly as possible, assisting in securing Sunday school teachers, and addressing a dozen other pressing matters.

I remember how I grimaced when the receptionist at our business buzzed my phone to tell me the preacher was out front to see me. I didn't want to see him. What did he want now? Reverend Henderson was a wonderful pastor and good friend, so it wasn't anything personal. I simply hated the thought of doing more church work. I was busy in the company. Why couldn't he take care of the church?

Jesus had warned about trying to serve two masters. He said, "No one can be a slave to two masters. He will hate one and love the other; he will be loyal to one and despise the other. So it is with you—one cannot have both God and wealth as your master" (Matt 6:24). I tried to serve both. God was God, and business and money were also gods. In truth, I came to hate the church and the demands it made on me. I hated the meetings. I hated the work of keeping it going. I hated all that went with keeping up my "image" of being a Christian businessman.

In reality, one of my underlying reasons for working with the church was to create this image of myself among my friends and associates. In the culture of the United States, especially in the South, it is important to project a Christian image. The successful, wholesome young man is active in church. He is a "Christian." Thus, much of what I did for the church was for my own credit and praise. I wanted the correct image, but I wanted to acquire it in my leisure time—not at the expense of the company or my personal pleasure.

The church not only got the crumbs of my time and interest, it also got the crumbs of my money. When I made $60,000 a year in salary, I gave the church $40 a month. After my salary increased to $100,000 a year, I gave $80. I rationalized this tiny offering on the theory that a larger contribution would wreck the budget of the church!

In our age of unprecedented prosperity, we should give much more than the biblical 10 percent to churches and voluntary agencies that are concerned with ministering to the physical and spiritual needs of people. In my case, I could have been giving more, but I gave less than 1 percent! Years earlier, when I made only a fraction of $100,000 a year, I had given 10 percent or more to the church. As more money came to me, however, I constantly decreased the percentage of giving. A tenth of $100,000 is $10,000. I reasoned, "That's too much to give away! I'll keep most of the money now so I'll have more to give later."

More tragic than the front I put up in the church was the façade of my personal life. Under a thin veneer of honesty, respectability, and Christian character lay a pile of rottenness. I tried to hide it from my friends and associates and even myself, but it kept threatening to reveal itself.

Chapter 24

Life in the Bubble

I had promised in college that I would serve God, but shortly afterward I was engaged in questionable business practices. Dees and I needed lumber for repairs on the apartment houses we rented out. We would go to the building and grounds supervisor, get permission to take a few pieces of old lumber, and then actually take all we needed when no one was looking, new and used alike.

We were always honest and fair with our customers—that was good business. With suppliers it was another story. We once wrote up a contract with a printing company promising to buy from them for a period of years at a specified price. Knowing they intended to purchase equipment especially for our work, we deliberately "fixed" the contract so it could be broken if we were able to get a lower price from another printer before the contract term expired. If we secured a lower bid, we would then be in a position to force the company with whom we had a contract to reduce their price even lower in order to salvage their investment in the new equipment.

In my personal conduct, I developed a "regionalized Christianity." At home, I behaved according to accepted Christian standards—at least openly. But on my increasingly frequent trips to St. Louis, Chicago, New York, and other cities, I adopted another code of conduct. During the election campaign of 1958, while a student at the University of Alabama, I became West Alabama campaign manager for McDonald Gallion, who was then running for attorney general of the state. Even though I did not believe in segregation and discrimination, I spoke more than seventy times for Mr. Gallion to all-white groups, and in every speech I preached segregation. One of my speeches in Fayette, Alabama, was to a huge gathering of robed

Klansmen. The meeting took place in the county courthouse in the middle of town. There were so many Klansmen that night that they all could not get inside. A public address system was rigged so those outside could hear. My preaching against integration boomed out over several city blocks.

In my drive toward success in business and law—my unbridled quest for more and more money—everything was subordinated to the activities that were fruitful to the realization of these goals.

I discovered that this drive has a way of separating man from God, from his family, and from his fellow man. The more money I made, the farther removed I seemed to become from people my own age. Either I didn't have time for them or they figured I was too far ahead of them for normal relationships. I kept hearing sarcastic quips: "What kind of racket do you have going now?" "If you're making all that money, you must be stealing it."

In college, I had promised God that I would share my money generously and not become selfish. But every higher plateau of affluence brought new appetites for more things for me. Nothing was ever shared.

When Linda and I dated during my law school days at the University of Alabama, I drove the old "company" panel truck. I borrowed a car to go on a three-day honeymoon. Soon after we married, I bought an old Ford car. At graduation we traded it for a newer Chevrolet. Then, shortly after getting to Montgomery, we bought a brand new Ford. Soon we got a second car—a new Buick. By 1964, we were driving a Lincoln Continental.

After we married, we lived first in one of our two-room student apartments at the university. Next, we moved into a three-room house in Lawton, Oklahoma. When we relocated to Montgomery, Alabama, we rented an apartment. Within two months, we purchased a four-bedroom, two-bath house. We bought secondhand furniture for our basic needs. As more money became available, we got rid of the old furniture and filled the house with expensive new pieces. We did extensive remodeling, including plush carpets, fancy wallpaper, and custom drapes.

By 1965, though, we were no longer satisfied with that house. We wanted something bigger. We purchased a twenty-acre parcel of land in an exclusive section just east of the city and hired an architect to draw plans for a $150,000 house. Our new home would include a big barn and pasture for saddle horses.

We already owned several riding horses in partnership with Dees. They were out in the country on our three cattle farms that totaled more than 3,000 acres. Our insatiable desire for land was somewhat like my other appetites for more and more of whatever we were buying. To begin with, we bought a 300-acre farm, then 500 additional acres, then 1,500 more. Someone remarked one day, "You fellows don't want all the land in the world. You just want all that joins yours!"

We bought a cabin on Lake Jordon, near Montgomery, and two speedboats. Then I traded one of the boats for a much larger one. Linda and I were well-to-do by this time, but our marriage was on the decline. Though we still slept in the same bed, it was so big that we didn't even need to know the other one was there! She had her car and I had mine. We had a domestic employee who worked fulltime Monday through Friday. She cleaned house and cared for our two preschool children. In fact, we had just about everything, but we were losing the most important ingredient to any marriage—love.

I was losing my capacity to love or be loved. I was a stranger to my children. Success in business had cost me dearly. I had gained money, prestige, and material possessions—an expensive home, furniture, boats, cabin, horses, land, cars. What had I lost? My wife, my family, my friends, my early purpose of life, and faith itself.

I was also losing my vigorous health. On April 8, 1964, I wrote about this problem in my diary: "My neck has been hurting for a week. I would like to know what is the matter with it. I haven't been well for three weeks. First, my kidneys got out of whack. Then I had headaches. Then my neck started hurting. About four days ago my back ached. Now my neck has started hurting again. I'll be glad to get back into 100% good health."

Shortly thereafter, I developed a severe breathing problem. My chest felt as if a tremendous pressure were bearing down on it. I frequently gasped for breath. Hundreds of times, I grabbed hold of the arms of my chair and struggled to fill my lungs with air. Often, I had to leave my desk and walk around the office or around the outside of the building in order to relax enough to resume normal breathing.

A few people saw what was happening to me. My father issued a warning several times. Others dropped hints from time to time that I might be heading for trouble. One day, Donald Moore, the cousin with whom I had sold mistletoe, visited me at the office. He asked me to step outside with him. On the lawn in front of the building he stooped down, pulled off a blade of grass, and started chewing on it. I squatted beside him.

"What is it, Donald?" I asked.

"I don't know how to say this," he started, "but I think you're off on the wrong track. Haven't your values gotten out of perspective in the process of building up this business?"

I looked him straight in the eye and laughed.

But he was right. I was just not ready to admit it.

Meanwhile, the business continued to mushroom. On February 8, 1965, I noted in my diary, "Business is good. We had the best single day of business today that we've ever had." By late February, only eight months after the last expansion, I was writing about the need for more working space. This time we decided to construct a separate building behind the existing plant. The new facility would more than double the size of our existing space. Work started in late spring. Before completion in the fall, we had to rent a large portion of a building in another part of town to accommodate a burgeoning work force. When we finally moved into the new plant, it was already too small. Immediately, we started to draw plans for another expansion that would double the size of the plant that had just been doubled!

Nearly all our products were exceeding projections in sales and profits, and new promotions were on the horizon that promised to eclipse the fantastic performance of those that preceded them. By late 1965, we employed 150 people, and sales were in excess of three million dollars a year.

The business was a success beyond my expectations. I should have been pleased and happy. Instead, I was anxious, depressed, and nervous. I felt something was wrong—that my life was heading toward disaster, but I couldn't afford to change anything. I had too much to lose. I continued working long hours and struggling to breathe. My personal problems, I thought, were simply part of the price one has to pay for "success," for "getting ahead."

Voices around me kept reminding me, "You've got it made. You're doing great. How many people would like to have what you have? You're on top, man, and going higher! Keep going." I reasoned, "Your marital problems will eventually resolve. Your breathing will soon return to normal. You'll feel better in a little while. Get the business built up. In a few years, you can hire someone to worry about it. You'll *really* have it made, then, and can do what you'd like."

I kept pushing.

Chapter 25

Dreams Becoming Nightmares

On a Saturday night in early November 1965, I was sitting on the side of our king-sized bed at home preparing to retire for the night. Linda walked in and sat beside me. Almost immediately I could tell something bothered her. She fiddled with her fingers momentarily and gazed at her lap.

"What's the matter, sweetheart?"

She looked up suddenly, right in my face. "How do you know you love me?" Her face was ashen, the corners of her mouth twitching.

"I just love you, that's all. I love everything about you. I—"

She didn't let me finish. "I have decided to go away for a while," she said. "I don't know if we have a future together. I want to think over a lot of things."

I was speechless. When Linda came into my office a year and a half earlier to announce that she didn't love me anymore and begged me to stay home some in the evenings, I had been shocked. But I thought we were getting past that problem now. In recent weeks, she had been telling me she loved me again.

Of course, I hadn't changed one iota in the way I worked or behaved toward my family. I continued to work from early in the morning until ten or eleven o'clock at night. We rarely had time together. We never went on vacation, but I thought she understood. She had been attending nearby Huntingdon College as a fulltime student and was extremely busy herself. She had completed requirements for her college degree in June, and I felt we were on the road to recovering the spark in our marriage.

Now this.

I tried to dissuade her, but she was insistent. She had to talk to someone, she said, and because you don't "hang out dirty linen" in your hometown, she was going to New York to talk to Dr. Lawrence Durgin, pastor of the Broadway United Church of Christ. We both knew Dr. Durgin. When I stayed in New York in 1963 working on the book *Off to College,* Linda and our two children were with me part of the time. We attended Dr. Durgin's church three or four times while living in the city.

On Sunday, right after lunch, Linda drove to the airport in her car and caught a plane to New York. I took the children in my car and drove out to one of our farms. I was left alone with our two children—Chris, age five, and Kim, age three—and alone with myself to think.

The next week was the loneliest, most agonizing time of my life.

At the company, I couldn't stay in my office alone. I had wanted to review our projects with key personnel in the company and plan sales strategies for the coming year. I arranged for all department heads to meet me on Lake Jordon at our cabin to talk over the phases of company activity. We met there every day that week, and I talked and talked and talked, trying to keep my mind off my marriage that was tottering on the brink of failure. I did not breathe a word to anyone about my personal problems. It would be bad for the company if employees were upset over my marital difficulties.

At five o'clock each afternoon—instead of my usual ten o'clock or eleven o'clock at night—I went home to relieve our domestic help. I took Chris and Kim for walks. I tried to play with them, but my heart wasn't in it. I gave them baths, searched drawer after drawer for clothes and pajamas, brushed little teeth, and tucked them in bed at night.

One evening, as I pulled the cover over Chris, he looked up at me in the dim light of his room and said softly, "Daddy, I'm glad you're home."

Chills ran up my spine because I knew that I had not been at home much except to sleep. Many mornings I left for the office before they awakened and came home after they had gone to sleep. I suddenly realized that I had become a stranger in my own household.

As I lay in bed each night tossing and tumbling, unable to sleep, I did a lot of thinking. How had this happened? How had I failed? Why wasn't Linda happy? She had everything a woman could want. What could I do now?

Linda and I had met in her hometown of Tuscaloosa when I was a law student. I was selling ads for one of our desk pads and walked up to the ticket window of the Druid Theatre downtown.

"Is the manager here today?" I asked the attractive young lady selling tickets.

"Yes," she responded.

"May I speak to him, please?"

"He's inside right now previewing a film. If you will wait a few minutes, I'm sure he'll be glad to see you."

"Okay, I'll wait."

As I stood there by the ticket window, I struck up a conversation with her. Finally, I asked, "What's your name?"

"Joan Caldwell."

I was forming my lips to ask for her telephone number when the manager walked up.

"I'm the manager," he said. "What can I do for you?"

"I would like to step into your office." As I walked away with him, I looked over my shoulder and smiled at my new friend. She smiled back.

I didn't sell an advertisement to the theatre that day, but that didn't matter. I wanted to get out of there and see the ticket seller again. When I finally walked back out front, a long line was in front of her window. I decided to run home and call her.

As soon as I got in my room, I dialed the theatre.

When a lady answered, I asked, "Is this Joan? Joan Caldwell?"

"No, she's not here. She's gone home."

"What's her phone number?"

"I can't give it to you. It's against theatre rules."

"Let me speak to the manager."

He answered. I told him what I wanted. "Sorry," he intoned, "it's against our policy and I can't help you."

I hung up, exasperated. I wanted to talk to Joan Caldwell right now. I opened the phone book and found about thirty Caldwells listed. I decided I'd start calling until I found Joan.

I dialed the first number. A girl answered. Aha, I thought, success right away!

"Are you Joan Caldwell?"

"No."

"Do you know her?"

"No."

"Thank you."

I dialed the second number. Another girl answered.

"I'm trying to locate Joan Caldwell. Do you know her?"

"No"

I dialed the third number. Another girl answered!

"Surely you are Joan Caldwell."

"No, I'm not."

"Do you know her?"

"She's a little older than me, so I don't know her well."

"Well," I begin to explain, "I've been trying to locate Joan Caldwell for an hour, but I'm ready to give up."

"Wait," she said. "I think I might find her phone number for you."

While she was trying to find the number, we started a conversation. We talked on and on. We discovered that one of my fellow law students was a member of her church. Finally, she asked how tall I was. "Six-four," I replied.

That was the final straw. She was five feet, ten and a half inches, and had been having trouble finding fellows tall enough for her. She became interested in meeting me. Within half an hour, I was standing in her living room looking at Linda Caldwell, my future wife.

I had fallen in love with Linda the moment I saw her that night.

On the first night of our married life, we signed what we named a "Resolution" in which we both promised to "out love" each other. Among other directives, we promised not to keep secrets from each other and to keep a "right relationship" with God. The week before we married, we wrote this Resolution together—she would write one word and then hand me the pen to write the next. We framed this agreement and hung it over our bed at every place we lived. During that week of sleepless nights, I wondered when we had stopped living by our "Resolution."

Chapter 26

Answering Another Call

While Linda was in New York, I thought about what we had vowed to do and not to do. I got the Resolution off the wall and read it again and again. We promised to love each other, and now she was off in New York City thinking about whether we had a future together, and I was in Montgomery, miserable and desperate.

By week's end, I was about to climb the walls. Linda had called on Thursday to say that I should come to New York the following Tuesday. The bottom of my heart almost fell out when I got this call. I wanted to go up there immediately or have her come back home. I could not bear the thought of staying in the house over the weekend. The term "a breaking heart" is a cliché, but it accurately describes my condition at that time. I was utterly desperate and lonely.

On Friday, I phoned Jim Hart, an employee of our company who was also a pilot. He was a young man who had recently joined the company as sales manager.

"Jim," I said, "I want to go on a trip this weekend. If I rent a plane, are you free to go?"

"I suppose so," he answered. "Where do you want to go?"

"Let's go to Niagara Falls. I haven't been there. On Monday we can hop over to Watervliet, New York, to see the people at the Tek-Hughes Plant about manufacturing some toothbrushes for us, and then go on down to New York City on Monday night. Linda has been there for a week. I'm going to meet her and we'll come back home together a couple of days later. You can fly home Monday night or Tuesday morning."

Darkness Falls

As the plane lifted from the runway toward New York, I felt good being alone. The responsibilities of being a wife, mother, and student had given me little time for personal care and reflection. During my week in New York, when I wasn't meeting with Dr. Durgin, I spent time either in my hotel room reading the Bible, meditating, and praying, or I ate in fine restaurants and went to museums, theaters, concerts, and elegant department stores.

Late one afternoon, I was in the prestigious Saks Fifth Avenue department store when the lights suddenly went out. Emergency lights flickered on, and clerks began urging customers to exit by way of the stairs. When I stepped onto the sidewalk, the only lights came from passing or parked cars. The streetlights were dark. Skyscrapers looked like giant shadows. I saw groups of people gathered around car radios to find out what was happening. People, even perfect strangers, were actually talking to one another—not typical in New York City. The news was a major power failure along much of the east coast. Restoration of service could not yet be determined.

Fortunately for me, I was only ten blocks from my hotel. As I entered the lobby, I saw a great throng of people solemnly milling around. I joined the cue to use what I learned was the only available telephone line. I had asked Millard not to call me until I had reached a decision. However, this unusual event merited a call to him.

He had learned about the blackout on the evening news and was glad to know I was all right. The hotel clerk offered me a book of matches, and I made my way up fourteen flights of stairs to my room. After stumbling around to get myself into bed, I laid awake for the longest time listening to sirens and wondering what daylight would bring.

—Linda Fuller

"That sounds fine with me. Let me ask my wife if there are any conflicts, and I'll also need to check the weather reports for the weekend. Do you want me to reserve a plane for us?"

"Yes."

"When do you want to leave?"

"In the morning."

Jim got busy. He made all the arrangements about getting a plane. After finding no conflicts with family or personal plans, he chartered our plane. By late afternoon he announced that we were ready to go.

Beverly Dees, my partner's wife, and George Seitz, a salesman for a printing company we traded with, decided to go along.

I was up at the break of dawn on Saturday making final preparations to leave. Our plan was to fly our two children over to Cusseta, Alabama. My father and stepmother would meet us at the small airfield. We would leave the children and take off immediately for Niagara Falls.

The phone rang. It was Jim.

"Bad news," he said. "Visibility is so low at the airport that we can't take off. In fact, it looks like we won't be able to take off any time today."

My heart hit rock bottom again. I hung up the phone and started pacing the floor wringing my hands. I called Jim again.

"Let's drive the kids over to Cusseta today. Then we'll be ready to go first thing in the morning. While we are over there we can go rabbit hunting for a while." He agreed and said he'd be over in an hour.

At Cusseta, we trouped through briar patches all afternoon looking for rabbits. I never slowed for a minute. The other hunters in our party began to comment that I was jumping more rabbits than the dogs! I pushed myself in order to become extremely tired. I hoped to be able to sleep that night. Tomorrow we would fly to Niagara Falls.

The next morning Jim checked the weather and reported to me that, unfortunately, the weather had become inclement.

"Let's go on out to the airport anyway," I said. "Maybe the situation will improve later in the morning."

I called Beverly and George and told them to drive over and meet us there.

After five hours of waiting, we finally took off sometime in the early afternoon. I was glad to get in the air.

The flight was without incident until we were a few miles south of Buffalo, New York. There, late in the afternoon and only a few minutes from our destination, we ran into a dark bank of clouds. Jim went strictly to instrument control of the flight.

All of a sudden, the altimeter went out. Ice began to accumulate on the wings. The radio started to sputter. There was dead silence in the cockpit. Jim worked feverishly with dozens of knobs on the instrument panel. Just then, an excited voice broke in between sputters on the radio to ask if we saw the DC-7 right under us. We didn't see it, but in our throats we felt it. All my problems came close to being solved—permanently!

A sigh of relief went up when we eventually emerged from that dark cloud bank and saw the city of Niagara Falls sprawled out beneath us.

On the ground, four relieved people emerged from the plane. Jim explained the seriousness of the problem we lived through in the cloud bank. We were glad the adventure had ended.

From the airport we took a taxi and drove into Canada to find a hotel for the night. We soon found a suitable one near the falls, rented two rooms, and got ready for dinner. Beverly had a room down the hall from the room where Jim, George, and I were staying.

While we dressed, Jim reached down and turned on the TV. A movie was in progress about a young woman who had gone to China as a missionary. She worked with children in an orphanage. Soon after arriving there, she met a young officer in the Chinese army. They fell in love. The young officer wanted to marry this American missionary woman, but he knew if he did, it would wreck his career in the Chinese army. With this dilemma facing him, he went to see the village leader—a Mandarin—to seek his advice. He told this goateed, wrinkled old man of his plight. The old man listened attentively and then, with the camera zooming in on his face, gave this advice: "A planned life can only be endured."

I don't remember what was said after those words were spoken because they put my mind in a whirl. The words leaped out of that television as if God himself had spoken them directly to me.

This young officer was living a planned life. Every stage of his life from youth until retirement was mapped out, and the old man told him such a life could only be endured. I was living the same kind of life. My overriding goal was to keep building up the company to make more and more money. The final stage of my planned life was to be buried in the rich section of the Montgomery cemetery.

"A planned life can only be endured. A planned life can only be endured." These words echoed over and over again in my ears. Was God really speaking to me through that movie?

The next morning, we spent a couple of hours looking around the falls. Then we caught a cab back to the airport, climbed into the plane, took off for Watervliet and the meeting with representatives of the Tek-Hughes Plant. By late afternoon, the meeting at the plant had ended and we were winging our way south to New York City.

The closer we came to landing, the more nervous I grew. What was going to happen? Would Linda and I be reconciled to each other, or would this be the end of our marriage? What did the future hold for me? For us? These questions pounded ever harder in my head as we sailed our way to the nation's largest city. As we approached LaGuardia Airport, the ground below became one huge sea of lights—millions and millions of lights. The sky was crystal clear that night, and we could see for miles. I was awed by this tremendous spectacle. Truly it was magnificent beauty. But how small and insignificant we seemed in our little plane circling the airport among a dozen giant aircraft, suspended above so vast a sea of humanity and giant buildings!

Surely, I thought in a fleeting moment, a single man is a tiny creature. What is one person among all of this? Then I remembered the questions and thoughts of the psalmist: "What is man that thou art mindful of him? And the Son of Man that thou doest care for him? Yet thou hath made him a little less than God and doth crown him with glory and honor. Thou hath given him dominion over the works of thy hands; thou hast put all things under his feet. O Lord, Our Lord, how majestic is thy name in all the earth!" (Ps 8:4-9).

The previous week, for one whole night, these same lights that now glittered so brightly all around and below us were in total darkness. The symbolism of the coincidence of the blackout and the black period in my personal life did not escape me. As I pondered what a totally black New York must have been like, I remembered the "dark week" I had lived through in Montgomery and the darkness in my heart at this present moment.

Soon, the circling was over and our plane went in for a landing. The spectacular beauty of a million lights became the glare of a set of headlights and a line of dingy bulbs in a dirty corridor. Lights don't look so pretty up close.

I raced for a telephone. I had called Linda from Watervliet and told her I'd be in that night. She had said I should come on Tuesday, but I wondered if she would see me on Monday night. She had agreed. Now I wanted to tell her that I had arrived at the airport.

No answer. *Maybe she's in the lobby waiting for me. Yes, that's it,* I thought. *She's in the lobby. I must hurry. But what if she isn't in the lobby? Where is she? Did she decide to leave me? Has she already gone?*

It was sheer agony riding to the hotel. I was in a daze when the taxi driver finally announced, "Here's the Wellington, sir."

I paid him and got out. I wanted to go in, but fear gripped me. What would I do if she weren't there? I had been in a mad rush, but now that I was here, I walked in slowly.

And then I saw her across the room smiling, looking straight at me. She was dressed in a black dress, even prettier than the first day I saw her seven years earlier. I was happy—but sad, too. I smiled as my eyes filled with tears. She got up and walked toward me.

"Hi," she said. "How was your trip?"

I took her hand and pulled her close to me. We were back together again, and I was glad.

In the night and day that followed, we talked a lot. We also had a conference with Dr. Durgin the next morning. Linda said she wanted to try to make our marriage work. I wanted to be happy about this decision, but in my heart I knew something still stood between us. Our underlying problem, I knew deep inside, was yet to be solved.

Late in the afternoon, Linda said, "Let's go to a movie tonight."

"Okay," I replied. "What do you have in mind?"

"Well," she said, "There is one at Radio City called *Never Too Late*. Let's see it."

The title struck me as symbolic of Linda's and my situation— *Never Too Late*. Was God now speaking to me again through the title of a movie?

I went to Radio City that night expecting to see a serious movie, with possibly a high moral theme about it never being too late to change one's errant ways in life. But the movie was not serious at all. It was a story about the problems of a couple in their fifties when the wife got pregnant after they both thought it was too late. Linda and I laughed all the way through it. I had hardly smiled for a week, and it felt good inside to bounce a bit with laughter.

I'm sure God has a sense of humor. Even though the show was a comedy, it spoke to me just as the film did two nights earlier in Niagara Falls.

During intermission, Linda and I walked downstairs to the refreshment area of the theatre. We bought a couple of sodas and found seats in a nearby lounge area. We sat quietly, sipping our drinks, not saying a word. The sounds of laughter were gone by this time, and my heart was again heavy with worry and concern about the future.

I tried to act normal with Linda, but I was uneasy and awkward in her presence. Our smiles were forced—unreal. Both of us knew something still stood between us, and we realized, at least subconsciously, that these barriers had to fall if we were ever going to be truly reconciled. But when walls have been built between two people over a period of months or years, who has the courage to strike the first blow to knock them down?

A hundred thoughts spun in my head, and I know they did in Linda's, too.

Then I heard her begin to sob softly. I turned to comfort her. When my hand touched her shoulder, the sobs magnified.

"What's the matter?" I urgently asked.

She answered by crying louder.

Everything I said or did had the same result: more crying.

Finally, I said, "Let's get out of here." To this, she assented by nodding and reaching for her coat.

We hurried out into the chilly, damp night, leaving behind our unfinished drinks, an umbrella, and the movie. Our urgent business was to tear down some ugly walls, but we didn't know how to start. Neither of us spoke. We continued walking in silence—block after block. Maybe we walked for an hour. I don't know. When we came to St. Patrick's Cathedral, floodlights beamed on the magnificent white structure. We sat on the steps to rest and started to talk. There seemed to be warmth in our tone, like more of a closeness developing. We began to talk about subjects that mattered. We talked about things that were separating us and had been stored up for months.

Never Too Late

I poured my heart out during my sessions with Dr. Durgin. All my pent-up hurts and feelings of loneliness and disappointment came rushing out. He leaned back in his chair and listened. I met with him every day for a week.

I actually considered filing for divorce. I thought it impossible for Millard and me to rekindle our love for each other, although that was my biggest hope. Money, cars, and clothes no longer mattered—not even the mansion we were planning to build. As the thought of it flashed through my mind, all those rooms seemed more like a prison than a place for raising a family.

In my last session, Dr. Durgin reviewed what he had determined were my options. He ended by saying, "If you loved each other once, you can love again." This gave me hope as he explained that the final choice was mine and that he had no intention of telling me what I should do. It was scary. I was aware that my life literally hung in the balance, and I was in agony over the choice I needed to make. I returned to my hotel room and fell on my knees, pleading to God for direction.

The previous afternoon, I had received word from one of Millard's secretaries that he was on his way to New York. I was excited to see him and waited for him in the hotel lobby. When he came through the revolving door, I didn't recognize him at first because I expected him to come bounding in at his usual breakneck speed. Both of us were at a loss for words, and the awkwardness I felt was more intense than if I had just met a stranger. We stepped onto the elevator.

I shared with Millard about my talks with Dr. Durgin. Millard listened, but it was as if he were in a fog. We decided to catch the last show at Radio City Music Hall. One of the features was titled Never Too Late. *That sounded appropriate, so we purchased tickets and slipped into one of the balconies since the movie had already started.*

As the story progressed, it became obvious that it did not parallel our situation at all. It was about a couple in their mid-fifties who became pregnant after both thought they were past that probability. During intermission, we went downstairs for refreshments. All of a sudden, I was no longer interested in staying for the stage show. I felt an urgent need to leave the theater. Millard and I walked for several blocks before I could stop crying. It was as if time stood still.

We passed exquisite shops on Fifth Avenue and Rockefeller Plaza. Magnificent jewelry that I could have purchased without considering the cost no longer appealed to me. I thought, Here I am, dressed in the most beautiful clothes money can buy, and yet I am miserable. *We were drawn to the lights flooding St. Patrick's Cathedral and seated ourselves on the front steps. Crying as much as talking, we started being completely open and honest with one another.*

> *I began to tell Millard about having an affair that he knew nothing about. I was afraid he would walk away and leave me forever. Instead, he grabbed me and held me close. We sobbed and sobbed. I asked him to forgive my unfaithfulness.*
>
> *It started to rain, and we hailed a taxi. On our way back to the hotel, we keenly felt God's presence bidding us to change our lives.*
>
> *The blackout in New York as well as the one in our lives was over! The light of truth and love flooded in. Darkness disappeared.*
>
> *—Linda Fuller*

Linda shared her disappointments in the marriage and I began to understand her pain and bitterness. The wall between us was beginning to crumble. Our walk continued over to Rockefeller Plaza. As rain started lightly falling, we ducked into the doorway of a little shop, held each other tightly, and cried our hearts out.

The flood of tears had a tremendous therapeutic effect. They seemed to cleanse and wash away so much that was staining and discoloring our lives. I held my hands around Linda's face and, looking straight into her eyes, told her how much I loved her. She knew I meant it.

She told me of her love for me, and from that moment on, a gradual reconciliation began to take place in our broken marriage.

It started to pour. I hailed a taxi and we headed to our hotel. Sitting in the taxi, holding Linda close to me, I thought of all that I had experienced in the past week—the power failure; the movie on TV with the message, "A planned life can only be endured"; the movie *Never Too Late*; and the new life that had just come to our marriage. I remembered the pressures that had built in me over the past months. I pondered the questions that had plagued me about whether I was using my life as I should. I thought about the business and all the time I had spent in building it. I thought about the goals in our business, the money we were making, and the money we planned to make. I thought about this and a lot more.

Then, all of a sudden, a strange calm came over me. I heard questions from somewhere—to me. It was the voice of God asking, "What are you doing to yourself? Where are you going? What is all this leading to?"

I answered, "It isn't leading me anywhere. I am willing to let go if you're willing to take over."

I immediately turned to Linda and related to her what I had experienced. I said I wanted God to take over our lives and our problems. Through the tears, a smile appeared. She gripped my hand hard and whispered, "Thank God. I feel the same way."

Chapter 27

Getting on the Road to Zion

Back in the hotel room, Linda and I decided to sell our interest in the company and our land, house, cabin, boats, horses—everything—and give away the proceeds to the poor. We felt that the material things and the drive to acquire them had pulled us apart, separating us from God and from each other. It was just that simple for us: get rid of them. We admitted failure and humbled ourselves before God to forgive us for our sins, and we resolved, with his help, to start over.

Months later, I told about this experience in a church in Riverside, California. At the conclusion of my talk, a young man came forward to ask about it.

"What happened in that taxi?" he inquired.

"Have you ever attempted to work a difficult math problem and it just seemed to defy solution?" I asked him.

"Yes," he replied slowly.

"And have you ever experienced the solution fairly leaping off the page at you, and then you wondered how you could ever have failed to see it sooner?"

"I sure have," he quickly responded. Then he turned and walked away. He knew exactly what I had experienced in that taxi and why we made our decision in the hotel room.

Linda and I continued to talk and cry and laugh and pray and sing until dawn. (We have often wondered what the hotel guests in adjoining rooms thought was going on.) One of the songs we sang and kept singing for weeks was "Marching to Zion." The direction of our lives had changed one hundred and eighty degrees, and our hearts were full of joy and praise.

We're marching to Zion. Beautiful, beautiful Zion.
We're marching upward to Zion, the beautiful city of God.
Come, we that love the Lord and let your joys be known.
Join in a song with sweet accord. Join in a song with sweet accord.
And thus surround the throne. And thus surround the throne.
We're marching to Zion. Beautiful, beautiful Zion.
We're marching upward to Zion, the beautiful city of God.

We experienced sadness over our failures and happiness because God's grace was sufficient to pull us from the pit of despair into which we had allowed ourselves to fall.

You're Going to Do *What?*

When Millard suggested selling his interest in the company and starting completely over again, I was amazed. Never in a million years did I dream he would give up what he had worked so hard to achieve. A new direction—leave business, leave Montgomery, sell or give everything away. As crazy as it seemed, it all started to make sense and feel like the right thing to do. My spirits began to soar and my mind begin to race with thoughts and questions. What will our parents think? My sister? Friends? People in the church? I thought how happy our children will be to have more time with their daddy. What will I do with all those clothes and shoes in my closet?

When Millard and I reflected on this amazing few days after returning to Montgomery from New York, we found it interesting the variety of ways people reacted to our big news. Understandably, most were shocked. My father, who had wanted to reach a higher pentacle of success in business, was one of the most shocked. He had been in awe of the rapid success his son-in-law had achieved. On the other hand, Millard's father, even though he was so proud of Millard's level of success, appreciated our drastic decision coming from the standpoint of faith.

Our friends' responses, after the initial shock subsided, were mixed. Some were sympathetic and understanding. Others tried their best to talk us out of it. I think a few people just couldn't deal with it and never made an effort to talk with us. False rumors began to circulate that Millard had had a mental breakdown and I was trying to get him committed.

In all the "craziness" we found ourselves in, we decided that we needed some time away with our children. In a way, it was a way to escape. However, the main reason was that we wanted some pure bonding time, both as a couple and as a family. Now we began to feel truly rich, and excitement filled us to the very core.

—Linda Fuller

I told Linda about the ways I had felt God leading us to our decision. I shared with her my thoughts on the significance of the movie I saw in Niagara Falls and the title of the movie at Radio City Music Hall. She then told me about a movie that had prompted her decision to come to New York. Earlier on the night she had sat on the edge of our bed in Montgomery and told me she was going away for a while, we had gone to see the movie *Ship of Fools*. The setting was a luxury ocean liner. As the story unfolded, Linda explained that she found herself identifying with characters who lived lives of "quiet desperation." She had come home that night feeling a great sense of urgency to make the changes necessary to get her life back on track

God does not deal with us in a vacuum. Rarely does he reveal himself to people through a "burning bush." Instead, he speaks to us where we are as we go about our daily activities, communicating through the medium of familiar things. God spoke to us through movies—funny and serious—and a power failure. But he can speak in many other ways, too. Sometimes we simply do not want to hear. We do not want to listen and heed.

The stage was beautifully set for me to leave the company. The week Linda was in New York talking to Dr. Durgin, I had met every day, reviewing our projects, with every department head. Detailed plans were laid for all phases of company activity during the next nine months. The significance of the timing of this planning was a powerful "coincidence." In my mind, it was just one more piece of evidence of God's hand in our situation.

The next morning, we decided to go to a fine restaurant to celebrate our renewed faith and love for each other. As we emerged from the side entrance of the Wellington Hotel, a taxi approached. I hailed it. The driver immediately pulled to the curb. As we were seated, he turned and said, "Congratulations!"

"For what?" I asked.

"This is a brand new taxi, and you are the first passengers to ride in it."

I looked at Linda. Her face beamed. She eased her hand into mine and squeezed hard.

"Driver," I said, "take us for a drive through Central Park. I've got a story to tell you."

For the next half hour, as we wound our way through the park, I leaned forward, placing my crossed arms on the back of the front seat, and told him of the many things that had happened to us in the last few days and about the decision we had made a few hours earlier to turn everything loose and let God run our lives. The taxi driver was deeply moved by our story, and talking to him meant a great deal to us. I do not remember his name, and he probably doesn't remember ours either, but he will never forget the first passengers in his new taxi.

Later in the day, I called Morris Dees, my business partner in Montgomery, and told him of our decision. He and I had made an agreement many months earlier that if either of us decided to leave the company, he would give the other an opportunity to buy his half of the interest. The next day, Dees flew to New York, and we began arrangements for him to buy my interest in the business.

It would take the next four months, and several conferences in Montgomery with attorneys and accountants, to work out a final settlement on all our jointly held properties, and a year to sell Linda's and my personal property—house, cabin, boats, land, etcetera—but we made plans that day to put the process in motion before doing anything else.

The next thing Linda and I did was go on a vacation with our two children—our first vacation as a family. We flew back to Montgomery, drove to Cusseta, picked up Chris and Kim, and headed for Florida. For nearly two weeks we meandered through the state, stopping wherever we fancied. Without fail, when we walked up to a new attraction—Weeki Wachee, Bok Towers, Cypress Gardens, or whatever—it was always just ten minutes until the next performance. We were constantly amazed at the timing of our totally "unplanned" vacation.

This time together as a family at the outset of a new direction in our lives was a thrilling experience for all of us. Linda and I continued to sing spontaneously. "We're Marching to Zion" was still our favorite. At night in the motel rooms, we told stories to the children. Linda and I read the Bible together and prayed. This was something we had never done before as a family, and it gave us strength for the uncharted days ahead.

Chapter 28

Turning on to Koinonia

As we drove north out of Florida after our vacation, I remembered my good friend, Al Henry, former pastor of the Pilgrim Congregational Church in Birmingham, who recently had moved to Koinonia Farm near Americus, Georgia. We decided to go to the farm to see Al and his family for a couple of hours. We ended up staying the whole month of December. There is no doubt that God led us there to begin preparing us for a new life in partnership with him and mankind.

Koinonia is a small, integrated community of dedicated Christian people who live together in much the same way as the early Christians did. They try to live out a Christian witness in everything they do, guided by three main principles: "Peace, Sharing, and Brotherhood."

Koinonia Farm was founded in 1942 by Clarence Jordan, who is still a member of the community and considered by all to be its spiritual leader.[1] In the beginning, people of Koinonia supported themselves by operating a poultry business. They sold eggs, smoked hams, produce, and other farm products at a roadside market on Highway 19, which at that time was the main north/south route to Florida. They had hundreds of customers. Even though Koinonia was interracial from its founding, the farm enjoyed good relations with the surrounding white community until 1954. After the famous desegregation case of that year, they had problems with the local whites. Representatives of the Ku Klux Klan visited them and issued an ultimatum for them to leave. The people of the farm refused. One night, a caravan of ninety carloads of Klansmen drove into the community in a show of force. Clarence Jordan met them and advised that they were wasting their time. "We are not leaving," Jordan told them.

A massive harassment campaign against the farm was instituted. For the next five years the community was constantly shot at, and several buildings burned, including the roadside market, which was blown up twice. Clarence Jordan's house was shot twenty-three different times. A total boycott was established throughout the county against Koinonia products. Most people in the county voluntarily stopped trading with the farm. They would neither buy nor sell. Those who did not stop trading with them had their barns burned down or threats made against their lives. Eventually, the farm lost every single customer. Their poultry business was wrecked. Some of the white families on the farm left under this constant pressure. All of the Negroes left because their relatives in the county were constantly being intimidated. Clarence Jordan and a handful of others remained and started the slow process of rebuilding. They were deeply in debt as a result of this trouble. How could they continue? No local business was feasible. Who would buy their products?

Someone came up with the idea of selling pecans and pecan products by mail. They located used pecan processing equipment and erected it on the farm, then began to solicit orders by mail from out of state. The motto was, "Help Us Ship the Nuts Out of Georgia." They tried mail-ordering smoked hams, but that item was problematic. Apparently, the aroma was too tempting along the shipping route, and most customers received the burlap sack without the ham.

Within a few years, the farm was back on the road to recovery. By the time of our visit, the community was almost out of debt and had a booming business of selling pecans, pecan candy, date pecans, and fruitcakes all over the United States and even in foreign countries. Their business, as a matter of fact, was one of our reasons for deciding to stay in December. They had difficulty shipping all orders promptly due to a shortage of help. As you can easily imagine, December was their busiest month for shipping fruitcakes, pecans, and candy for Christmas.

Our second reason for staying at Koinonia for a month was to grow spiritually. On the first day of our visit, we ate lunch in the community dining room with all the people at the farm, maybe twenty to twenty-five individuals. It was a time of fellowship and reporting of the day's news. After the meal, a few of us gathered around a table with Clarence Jordan and started talking.

A couple of men were there from Columbus, Georgia. (I later learned that one of them was a writer for a newspaper in Columbus. Before the discussion terminated, I talked about the experiences Linda and I had had during the past few days. He wrote an article about our conversation in the *Columbus Ledger-Enquirer* a few days later titled "A Rich Young Man Makes a Decision.") These men fired questions at Jordan about the purpose of Koinonia; about life; about the race issue; about war and peace; about Christ; and a dozen other subjects. Jordan's answers were quiet and deep. They spoke to me, and I felt strengthened simply by being there to listen and grow spiritually. I was tremendously stimulated by the experience and wanted to remain longer at the farm in order to pursue further some of the questions that had been raised. When we learned later in the day about the need for additional help with shipping, Linda and I decided to stay.

In the weeks ahead, we packed pecans, dates, and candy in the daytime and talked *all the time.* I helped in the warehouse with shipping, and Linda helped process orders in the office. I shared milking chores with Al Henry. We talked while we worked—on the way to town with a load of packages to be mailed, in the milking barn, walking to lunch, anywhere. At Koinonia, people are more important than pecans or money or getting shipments out. They sensed that we needed their encouragement and friendship, so they gave abundantly of themselves.

At the noon meal and at night, we talked in groups. Our subjects ranged from civil rights marches to the crucifixion to fruitcakes to the war in Viet Nam, but the common element running through all that was said and done at Koinonia was love. The people expressed an abiding concern for us as we prepared ourselves, emotionally and spiritually, for a new life.

We talked a lot about "success" and what it should mean to a Christian. Clarence Jordan pounded home the point that God calls us to faithfulness to God in order to achieve success. The world judges "success," but God judges our faith. He told about a news reporter who interviewed him one day during the height of trouble with the Ku Klux Klan. The reporter asked about the damage that had been done and the burden that rested on the community as a result of the boycott, the shootings, and the burnings. At the conclusion of the interview, the reporter asked, half sarcastically, "In summary, Dr. Jordan, how successful would you say Koinonia has been?"

His answer was classic. "About as successful as the crucifixion."

We discussed the incarnation quite a lot at Koinonia. With the smell of cow dung fresh in my nostrils from my morning and evening pilgrimages to the barn to milk the cow, I heard Clarence Jordan reminding us that Christ was born in a dirty stable. He lived the life of a poor boy, and throughout his ministry he lived and taught among the poor. Finally, he died an ignoble death on a cross between two common thieves. His birth, life, and death were filled with dirt, stench, poverty, suffering, and an agonizing death. "The trouble with so many Christians today," Jordan reminded us, "is that they try to push Christ back up into heaven. We like a nice *clean* Christ, replete with white robes and a golden cross. But if we would serve God, we must do it in the world. We must meet and serve people where they are—just as Christ did in his ministry."

There is a saying, "When the student is ready to learn, the teacher appears." Clarence Jordan became my teacher and mentor. He put me on course for the rest of my life.

Note

1. Clarence Jordan died suddenly of a heart attack on October 29, 1969.

Chapter 29

Encounters

"You cannot serve God and mammon (wealth)" was a common theme of our talks at Koinonia. Clarence Jordan called people who put things of the world first in their lives "mammon disciples." He was always telling stories to illustrate a point.

He told about a man in a nearby town who refused to sell fertilizer to one of the people from the farm because he felt it would hurt his business. Clarence, whom everyone called by his first name even though he earned a Masters in Divinity and a Doctorate in Greek New Testament, went to this man who happened to be a leader in his church and asked him about the refusal. The man restated his position that it would seriously hurt his business. Clarence asked the man if he thought it right to refuse to sell to a fellow Christian. He replied that it was not right and that he would do it if only . . . . Clarence stopped him to ask, "What is really taking first precedence in your life? God or your business?" The man would not answer because he knew what he would have to say. He professed to be a Christian, but God came second.

At times like these, if God is not in reality first in our lives, we despise him for making such a preposterous claim on us. We actually hate God for demanding so much. In the words of Christ, "No man can serve two masters; he'll hate one and love the other; he will be loyal to one and despise the other. So it is with you—you cannot have both God and mammon (wealth) as your master" (Matt 6:24).

During our month at Koinonia with Clarence relating story after story, I never heard one word of bitterness expressed toward the Ku Klux Klan for the physical damage they did to the community, but Clarence had harsh words for many of the established church leaders in the area. He talked about them in the context of the commandment, "Thou shalt not take the name of the Lord in vain" (Deut 5:11). "Most Christians," he said, "limit the meaning of this commandment to swearing, but the larger and the more serious offense against the commandment is to 'take' the name of the Lord into one's life and profess to be God's servant while continuing to live as in the past. A person who 'takes' on God's name in such a case has taken it in vain. It is just like a woman who marries a man, takes his name, and then is unfaithful to him. She has taken his name in vain."

"Churches also take God's name in vain," he continued. Clarence refused to call them "churches." Rather, he called them "God boxes." "A group of people get together," he explained, "erect a building, write up some rules about the kind of God they want to live there, and then invite him in. The trouble is, he doesn't come. A house of God cannot be operated by any rules but God's rules."

Clarence told a story about a young man from India who visited the farm during the early years of its existence. The young man was not a Christian, but he was curious to learn about the faith. Dr. Jordan talked with him at length. When Sunday came, he expressed an interest in attending church with them. At that time, the Jordans attended a nearby Baptist church. Dr. Jordan told the young man they would be glad to have him attend with them. Upon their arrival for worship, the church officials barred entry to the young man because his skin was a dark brown.

Later that week, the church informed Dr. Jordan that his family had been "thrown out" for attempting to bring that man to worship. Dr. Jordan demanded an explanation of this action from the board of deacons. A special board meeting was called, and Dr. Jordan appeared with a Bible. Handing it to the first man, he asked them to give their biblical basis for their action against him and his family. The first deacon handed the Bible to the second deacon, and he to the third, and so forth, until the last man at the end of the table received it. He fumbled with it momentarily, then cast it aside with the comment, "We'll not talk about that. We're just not having any niggers in our church!" The visitor was not a Negro, but to them that was immaterial. He was dark skinned, and their church rules called for white Christians only.

From that time on, worship services were held on the farm each Sunday. These services were open to anyone who wanted to come, whether white, black, brown, or yellow; whether from Georgia, Maine, California, or Montana; whether from Africa, Brazil, Australia, or India. God's church at Koinonia is still open to all of God's children.

We found the Sunday morning "church" program at Koinonia to be a highlight of the week. Early in the morning, Al Henry would get into the farm Volkswagen bus and drive through the surrounding countryside to pick up children for Sunday school. Every time the bus drove back through the farm gate, little black smiling faces peered from every window. When the last load arrived, the community farm bell was rung, Koinonia residents stepped from their houses, and everybody gathered in the community dining hall. Someone would slide up to the old piano, and we'd sing a few familiar hymns.

After that, Clarence would tell an installment of the story about Moses and all his problems with Pharaoh. The children (adults, too) would sit spellbound for thirty minutes while he thundered and gestured his way through. Whatever those children do later in life, I am positive they will never forget Moses and Pharaoh and all the other Bible characters Dr. Jordan told them about in such an interesting and exciting way.

Following the story, the assembly divided into smaller groups for another forty-five minutes of planned activity with the children and a Sunday school lesson delivered to adults and older youth by someone in the community. Our final activity of the morning was a freewheeling discussion group among the adults about anything anyone wanted to talk about.

No one dressed up for "church." We wore overalls, boots, jeans—whatever we would wear any other day of the week. This attribute of the Koinonia "church" disturbed my family when they visited us one Sunday. I'm sure it would disturb others, but where in the Scriptures does one find the commandment, "Wear a suit and necktie to church"? What makes us think that expensive clothing is pleasing to God or that failure to wear fine clothing to church is disrespectful to God?

One Sunday night during our stay at Koinonia, we attended another church for a special Christmas program. That was an exciting time. The story begins at a noon community meal at the farm. Carol Henry, Al's wife, announced that her father was going to be in town the following day to preach at the First Baptist Church of Americus. Carol's father is a well-known Baptist preacher in South Georgia. She showed us an advertisement in the local paper about the service. It stated that the "public is invited."

The next day, Carol's father came to our community lunch. During sharing time, he made kind remarks and issued an invitation for us to come to the church that evening. A number of us decided to attend.

Our group formed a line to enter the door of the church. We filed by several men who were handing out programs. Clarence entered first, then Linda and me, then Collins Magee, a Negro who worked at the farm in the afternoons after school. A program was automatically handed to Collins, but when the usher noticed that his hand was black, he froze. Greg Wittkamper, Carol, and Al, who came next, were not given a program even though they were white. When it was clear that all had gotten past the door, the group walked down the aisle nearly midway, found a vacant pew, and sat together. The congregation was singing "Gloria in Excelsis Deo." Hardly had we taken our seats when the people in the pew in front of us and the people behind us started whispering among themselves. The instant the congregation finished singing "Gloria," these two groups moved into the aisle and found seats elsewhere. This made an "island" of our Koinonia group, with vacant pews to the front and rear and aisles to the right and left. This, however, did not prevent us from joining in singing the next hymn, "It came upon a Midnight clear, that glorious song of old . . . peace on Earth, good will to men."

About halfway through the first verse, the frozen usher, now thoroughly thawed, came down the aisle and entered the pew in front of us. "He," he said, pointing to Collins, "can't stay in here!" When we ignored him and continued singing "peace on Earth," the usher said, glaring at Collins, "Am I going to have to drag you out of here? You're disturbing divine worship, and I'm going to have you arrested."

With this, the usher grabbed Collins, saying, "Come on, nigger, get out of here. You can't stay in here." The usher started to pull him across the bench.

Clarence stopped him and asked, "Do you have the authority to do this?"

"Yes."

"May we see the pastor?"

"No. You've got to get out of here. You're disturbing divine worship."

While the congregation was still singing about "peace" and "goodwill toward men," our entire group moved into the aisle and went out the door.

Standing on the steps outside with about a dozen laymen and the pastor standing between us and the door, the head usher told us, "This is our church. We own it, and we control it. The federal government didn't put one dime in it and can't tell us who we can let in."

Clarence said he thought the Holy Spirit controlled the church, and the reply was, "That's beside the point. This is *our* church. We own it."

"But doesn't God own the church?" Clarence pressed.

"I told you that is beside the point."

The pastor said he and some others didn't personally agree with this policy of turning Negroes away, but that the church had adopted it and it would be best for us to leave.

I piped in, "But Pastor, this woman's father is the guest preacher tonight, and he invited her and the rest of us to come."

"No!" the pastor looked shocked. "He's not your father!"

Carol responded, "Oh yes, he is. He's been my father all my life!"

There was a moment of silence and no indication of the pastor or the ushers changing their minds. Carol continued by asking the pastor to please tell her daddy that she came to hear him but was turned away. He said he would.

We left.

1964—The Fuller
millionaires in
Montgomery,
Alabama

Early 1965—Millard
in New York City.

December 1965—Millard writing letters
at Koinonia.

1968—Fuller family at Koinonia.

August 1965—Millard and Clarence
Jordan.

Winter 1969—Millard
at Koinonia a few
weeks following
Clarence's death.

Part 4

Daring to Dream

Chapter 30

What Now?

During our month at Koinonia, I was often on the phone to Montgomery, working on the process of closing out my interest in the business and selling our personal property. I also started corresponding with several leaders in the United Church of Christ and various seminaries about possibilities for my future. At the time, I didn't know whether I would take a job or enter seminary. I wrote Jim Waery in Philadelphia and told him I would soon be ready to take that trip overseas to visit missionaries. I arranged a series of meetings in New York and Philadelphia for mid-January for the purpose of exploring options about work (or seminary) and the trip to Africa.

A few days after Christmas, we waved goodbye to our friends at Koinonia who had become so much a part of us in such a short time, and we headed for my parents' home in Cusseta. Linda and I were convinced that our visit at Koinonia was providential. It was a rich experience for the whole family and a spiritually strengthening one for Linda and me.

My parents lived in an old two-story farmhouse that was in desperate need of repair, without adequate heating or decent drinking water. We had the joy of repairing their house—putting in a new furnace, digging a new well, and replacing their furniture with pieces from our house. We remained in Cusseta until mid-February, with a week out for a trip to New York and Philadelphia to talk about future plans.

The New York trip was a continuation of the exciting adventure of the past few weeks. Linda and I talked to the president of the United Church of Christ, Dr. Ben Herbster, an official at the church's Boards for Homeland Ministries and World Ministries. I talked to people at Union Theological Seminary. We considered and prayed about my working with the Homeland Board as an attorney; taking a mission assignment in Africa as a business manager of a hospital; attending seminary; and working as a fundraiser for Tougaloo College, one of our church-supported predominately Negro colleges located in Jackson, Mississippi. We talked with World Ministries Board personnel about the trip to Africa to visit missionaries and about speaking throughout the United States upon our return. It became a question of when and also making arrangements for ou rtwo children while we were away for seven weeks. We went by train to Philadelphia and conferred with Jim Waery of our UCC Stewardship Council concerning the Africa trip he had first proposed to me nearly two years earlier.

After the meeting with Waery, we returned to New York, where we had a second conference with people at the World Ministries Board about going to Africa. As we prepared to depart New York on the following morning for our return to Alabama, we were excited about everything that was opening up for us.

At Kennedy Airport, Linda and I entered into another of God's dramas that was clear evidence to us of his leading our lives. It began to unfold as we approached the gate just outside the plane we were to board for Atlanta, Georgia. A young African man, replete with native robes and a turban, sat there reading a newspaper. With the excitement of our forthcoming trip to Africa, I felt a strong urge to speak with him. Linda and I sat nearby, and I cast frequent glances in his direction. Finally, Linda punched me while I was engaged in one of my stares and whispered, "Go on over and introduce yourself. You won't be satisfied until you do."

I got up and walked over.

"Pardon me. I am Millard Fuller. My wife and I have been admiring your attire. Where are you from?

He looked up with a big smile on his face. "I am from Nigeria," he replied in crisp British English. "My name is Daniel Offiong."

He seemed thoroughly pleased that I had introduced myself. I sat beside him. In the next few minutes, I learned that he had just arrived in the United States and was on his way to Birmingham, Alabama, to enroll there at Miles College. I was the first American to greet him. He wore only his traditional dress without a coat. No one had told him it was cold in the United States in January. That morning in New York, it was nine degrees!

The call soon came for boarding the plane. I said goodbye to my new friend and rejoined Linda. We went on board and found our assigned seats. A few minutes later, I looked around, and right behind us sat Daniel Offiong. "He's in the seat behind us," I whispered to Linda. "Maybe God wants us to say something else to him. As soon as we are in the air, let's move back there and talk with him some more."

In the continuation of our conversation, we learned that he did not know anything about American currency, so I had the pleasure of teaching him about nickels, dimes, quarters, and dollars. He was full of questions about America, and we were delighted to answer as much as we could.

We discovered that he came from a large family. Polygamy is practiced in Nigeria (as in most parts of Africa), and his father had three wives and twenty-three children. Three years earlier, Daniel had been awarded a tuition scholarship to Miles College on the basis of his excellent marks in secondary school. He was preparing to leave for the United States when his father fell ill. It became Daniel's responsibility, as eldest son, to support the family. He moved from his tribal homeland in the eastern part of the country to Lagos, the capital of Nigeria, where he secured work first as a federal produce inspector and then as a sales clerk in a department store. For three years he worked at an average salary equivalent of $50.00 a month. Out of this money he supported his father's family and managed to save $180.00.

Finally, he felt he could leave his family to support themselves. He secured a loan of $840.00 from a credit union in his village, bought eighteen $10.00 American Express Travelers checks with his $180.00 savings, and headed for America and a college career.

There he sat beside us with $180.00 cash (he showed me his eighteen American Express checks) and a tuition-only scholarship. Why had he come to America with such meager resources? I asked a dozen questions about his background and about his motivation for seeking an education in America. Reluctantly, he told us of his difficulties in completing secondary school, having to help support his family, his dreams of a college education in the United States, his prayers, the faith others had in him, and his own unshakeable faith in God and his ability to accomplish the task he had set out to do.

I was impressed with his intelligence, determination, ambitions, and faith. Turning to Linda, I whispered, "If we've ever met anyone who needs help, it's this man. Let's give him some money. He doesn't even have a coat." Linda quickly agreed and she wrote a check for $50.00.[1] I handed it to him and said, "Here's a small gift we want to give you to help with your new life here in America." He took the check and looked at it for a long time. Then tears came into his eyes. Slowly he unbuckled his seatbelt, rose out of his seat, and bowed deeply to Linda and then to me. "Thank you, thank you," he whispered. He took his seat again and said he wanted to tell us a story. He gazed at the check as he talked.

"Last evening," he said, "I met with Reverend Mendie and several members of my church in Lagos. We kneeled and they all prayed for me. After this prayer service, Reverend Mendie put his arms around me and said, 'Daniel, I've got a prophecy to make. When you get to New York tomorrow, you're going to meet a Good Samaritan.'" At this point, Daniel looked up at us with tears now streaming down his cheeks. "Today," he said softly, "this prophecy has come true."

I stayed in touch with Daniel after our dramatic first meeting. He transferred to Tougaloo after one semester at Miles. There, he made an enviable record for himself. After graduation from Tougaloo, he planned to enter the University of Illinois and work toward a Ph.D. in Labor and Industrial Relations. Then he desired to return to his home country and work to build up his people.

Daniel is a dedicated Christian. Licensed to preach in the Christian Methodist Episcopal Church, he spends many weekends speaking in various churches in the Jackson area. He is an inspiration to fellow students at college and to all who know him.

I told Daniel's story to many people. Several made contributions to his education. Almost a year later, Jean Williamson, a fellow southerner from Mississippi who worked for *Newsweek Magazine* in New York, heard the story when I spoke to a young adult meeting at the

Marble Collegiate Church in New York City. Shortly afterward, she volunteered to head a drive to raise $20,000.00 for the Daniel Offiong Scholarship Fund at Tougaloo to provide a $1,000 scholarship each year to a worthy student.

Note

1. According to inflationdata.com, $50 in 1965 would have been worth approximately $330 in 2010.

Chapter 31

Giving It All Away

All of us have God-given opportunities to meet the needs of those around us. To receive the joy of sharing it, we must open ourselves to others—and in the process to God—and receive the gift of opportunity. Through experiences like the one with Daniel Offiong, I am continually discovering the truth in Jesus' words: "If you want to find yourself, you must lose yourself" (Luke 9:23-24).

Back in Alabama, I continued to work toward liquidation of our business and personal properties in Montgomery. By mid-February, the attorney had a stack of papers ready for us to sign. Linda and I spent half a day in the lawyer's office doing nothing but signing papers. It takes a lot of work to accumulate a lot of things, but it also takes work to get rid of them.

We gave away all cash payments from the sale of the business and all cash payments from the sale of our land, house, and cabin. We designated future proceeds from the sale of the business for various mission causes. The total amount of the settlement was approximately one million dollars. One hundred thousand dollars of our total estate went to pay certain obligations we had incurred. About thirty thousand went to my parents for repairs and remodeling of their home. We helped Linda's parents purchase an RV, which they had wanted ever since they retired a few years earlier. We set aside the remaining money for religious, educational, and other charitable causes.

I do not want anyone to conclude from this that people must do what Linda and I have done. I would never say to a businessman, "If you're making lots of money, you're wrong." All I would say is that *for me*, there was no other way. There was an albatross around my neck, and if I wanted to respond to God's call, I had to get rid of it. Perhaps giving it all away is the only way if you're addicted to making money.

It is possible to be wealthy and be a Christian, but it's my feeling—and my experience—that it is very difficult to do. Jesus said it is more difficult for a rich man to enter the kingdom than for a camel to go through the eye of a needle (Matt 19:23-24). He referred to a gate in Jerusalem that a camel could enter only if it were relieved of its load.

We can rationalize our desire for money by saying we're going to put God first. However, in my case, I became obsessed with making more and more money and left God on the sidelines.

I am not convinced that our American private enterprise system is wrong. Individual initiative is good and wholesome. I am still a champion of free enterprise. The high privilege of people realizing the fruits of their labors is not at all inconsistent with the will of God. The sin is in allowing wealth—or, for that matter, status, sex, power, prestige, or anything else in excess—to become a god.

Jesus said, "Seek *first* the kingdom of God, and all these things shall be added unto you" (Matt 6:33). I think the kingdom needs faithful and committed people—the minds, hearts, and lives of people. How much money did Jesus' disciples give to the kingdom? They gave *themselves* totally, just as Jesus had given himself, and they transformed their world. (If I make an impact on my world, it won't be through any money I give unless I can give myself in the process.)

By early February, Linda and I had made two decisions about our future. One, we would take the trip to Africa in the summer, and two, I would accept the job of development director for Tougaloo College. Even though the college is located in Mississippi, my office would be in New York City, because at that time the city offered more access to people of means as well as interest in supporting education for blacks. I would start work on April 1.

Linda wanted to make a final trip before settling down to our new assignment. She had a sister in California. Linda had been there once when Chris was less than a year old, but Kim and I had never been. In late February, we loaded up in a new station wagon I had acquired on a trade-in of the family car, and headed west. On the way out, we visited the Vicksburg Battlegrounds in Mississippi and toured Carlsbad Caverns in New Mexico. In Texas, we encountered unusual weather for that part of the country—a blizzard! Snow came down in sheets. It was difficult to see the highway, much less the painted lines. We practically froze. We thought we were going into warm weather, so we did not have any winter clothing with us. Our heaviest apparel was sweaters. We were one happy family when we *finally* reached Southern California.

The two weeks we spent with Charles and Janet Lawrence were a great time. We shared with them night after night all the experiences we had wept and laughed through in past weeks. Following one of our late-night sessions, Charles told me that for the first time since we had met, he felt that he really knew me and could be my friend. He said that when they had visited with us before, I always seemed too busy to be concerned with him—or with anyone else.

One night, the Laflin family—friends of the Lawrences—invited us to eat supper with them. Mr. Laflin owned one of the date-processing plants in the Cochella Valley, the heart of the date industry in the United States. During the evening, we talked about some of our experiences of the past weeks and especially about Koinonia Farm. I told Mr. Laflin about the pecan-stuffed dates sold by the farm. He said he had never heard of Koinonia, but he expressed interest in it.

The following morning, he phoned me at the Lawrence's home. "Guess what!" he exclaimed. "I received a letter in the mail this morning from Clarence Jordan of Koinonia Farm. He wants a quote on our dates." He was amazed at this coincidence fast on the heels of our conversation the previous night about Koinonia. I thought of the words of William Cowper's old hymn: "God moves in mysterious ways, his wonders to perform." What man of faith could doubt the imprint of God on this episode? A few weeks later, Koinonia placed an order for dates with Mr. Laflin.

From Indio, we drove south into Tijuana, Mexico, and then north along the scenic coastal route. We stopped in San Francisco for a couple of days to visit the sights around the city and take the kids for a ride on the famous trolley cars. One night, Linda and I decided to hire a babysitter for the children so we could go out for dinner and a tour of Chinatown. Upon our return, we learned that our baby sitter was a retired United Church of Christ missionary. We sat up with her until way past midnight talking about missionary work and mutual friends. She knew many of the people at our World Ministries Board and some of the missionaries we planned to visit in Africa.

Leaving San Francisco, we continued north to the Redwood Forest. At Eureka, we turned east through the mountains. Almost immediately, we encountered another blizzard, and I experienced some of the roughest driving I had ever faced. Rocks were falling off the cliffs, snow was coming in sheets, and visibility was almost zero.

On our return trip, we stopped by the Grand Canyon, traveled through the Petrified Forest, and saw the Painted Desert. In Lawton, Oklahoma, we visited the church we attended while we lived there for six months in 1960. All our friends happened to be at church that Sunday. In the afternoon, we had a great time riding around in the Wichita Wildlife Refuge and revisiting the site of the Easter pageant. I had played bit parts in the pageant of 1960. In the evening, our friends gave us a party.

From Lawton, we drove to Alabama in one long day, and from there to New York. All our remaining possessions went with us. We had given away everything that could not be packed into our station wagon. On April 1, I officially became an employee of Tougaloo College. The school was founded just north of Jackson, Mississippi, in 1869 by the American Missionary Association. It is church-related, yet open to all regardless of religion or race. A four-year fully accredited liberal arts college, Tougaloo is an educational institution dedicated to the task of adding substance to the belief that all are one under God and that there should be equal opportunity for all. Over the years, the school has struggled in the face of overwhelming odds to make this goal a reality.

My job with Tougaloo was to develop programs of support and solicit donations from churches, corporations, foundations, and individuals. These funds improved Tougaloo's academic programs and physical facilities on campus. The Development Office in New York was being opened to coincide with the launching of a $30 million, ten-year campaign.

Chapter 32

Another Step in the Right Direction

As a Southerner and a Christian, I was happy to take on this job at Tougaloo as a means of doing something concrete to improve the lot of my Negro fellow citizens. I used to think of Negroes as inferiors and saw nothing wrong in that view. When we discussed prejudice in Sunday school as children, we talked about how Indians were treated in New Mexico, or Japanese and Mexicans in California, but never about how Negroes were treated in Alabama.

I first met Negroes as equals through the nationwide conferences of our Pilgrim Fellowship. It was in these conferences, I am sure, that my attitude began to change. The seeds there took a long time to germinate, but by 1961 I was beginning to identify with the Negro's struggle for equality. In that year, the "Freedom Riders" came through Montgomery. I was at the bus station and witnessed their reception. It was a sad spectacle. I wrote about the event in my diary the next day:

May 22, 1961: The integrated "Freedom Riders" came into town on a Greyhound bus yesterday. They were met at the station by a mob. Two in the group were severely beaten. Newsmen and cameramen were also attacked and beaten. Police did not show up until twenty-five or thirty minutes after the violence had erupted. When they did come, they made no real effort to stop any mobsters. Later in the day, when the mob could not find the "Freedom Riders," they turned on innocent Negroes who were just standing around looking. They beat one old crippled Negro man. I think the action of this mob is senseless and utterly crazy. The action, or more correctly stated, the *inaction* by the Governor, the Sheriff, and the

Police Department is inexcusable. They could have, and should have, been present to prevent the violence that erupted. The fact that they condoned the action of the mob is clear evidence that the authorities here in the city have no regard for human rights unless it is connected with getting votes in the next election. We are in a sad state of affairs, but I am confident that the mob rule will be replaced in the near future and a man, or woman, regardless of color and regardless of the color of traveling companions, will be able to travel through our state in safety.

As a footnote of interest on how money took precedence over principle during this period in my life, a few days later our law firm took the case representing in court one of the men who had attacked several of the Freedom Riders. We accepted money from the Klan and White Citizens Council in payment of the fee for this man.

As time went along, however, I became more involved with the cause of the Negro. In 1963, at the Fuller & Dees Marketing Group, we hired a Negro to head our in-house printing operation. He became the first Negro in the city to hold such a high management position. That same year, we hired two students from one of the local Negro high schools to work part-time in the plant. In 1964, we recruited thirteen Negro high school and college students to work during the summer packing sample products for our fall mailings.

Soon after we hired these people, copies of the *Fiery Cross,* a publication of the Ku Klux Klan, were mailed to me and to our personnel manager. The copies were marked on the front in big letters: "PERSONAL." Our hiring of these people created a second minor problem. Some of the students were girls. It was the first time we had hired Negro women, and some of our white female employees objected to having coffee and going to the same rest room with them. Marilyn Black, our office manager, called a meeting to talk about the problem. A few people let off their steam, and that ended the matter.

Another "first" came at Christmas 1963. We announced that a Christmas party would be held at the Jeff Davis Hotel for "all employees." Most interpreted this to mean *all white employees.* When word got around that it meant *all* employees, whispering started. This time

I called a meeting of white employees, and we aired the situation. Afterward, it seemed that several people still did not intend to go to the party. Dees and I met individually with most of them. When the party was held, all white employees except three or four were present with their wives, husbands, or dates. All Negro employees came with wives, husbands, or dates. The Negroes sat at one table, but at least two of those couples danced during one of the numbers. There were no expressions of bitterness, and some of the white employees actually went out of their way to show friendliness to the Negroes. We were the first company in the city to have a party for employees and include the Negroes on an equal, integrated basis.

The famous Selma demonstrations and march to the capitol occurred in March 1965. I volunteered the use of my car and my services to drive marchers from Montgomery to Selma. I also offered our home to any marchers who needed a place to sleep. I made one trip to Selma with a load of ministers and several trips to the line of the march after it got under way. During the week, we hosted four marchers in our home.

This intense activity on behalf of "integrationists" incurred the wrath of my neighbors and people all over town. Our neighbors across the street stopped speaking to us, and the man of the house cursed me one morning as I got into my car. One night, an unidentified man called to threaten us for hosting the marchers.

The day the march ended at the capitol in Montgomery, I went to the city to observe. After returning to the office, I recorded my observations and feelings in my diary: "March 25: This past week was a full one. The big March from Selma climaxed in front of the Capitol. Police estimated that twenty-five thousand persons were in attendance. Dees and I got press passes and watched the event from right up front. It was quite a spectacle. I wanted to join the marchers and clap and sing right along with them, but convention held me back. I agree with this civil rights movement very strongly."

Within a matter of days, word was out all over town that I was a Communist. One story was that I printed Communist literature on a printing press in my basement. Another story was that Martin Luther King Jr. had stayed at my house. Several school and civic groups in the

city were selling our products, and most of them returned the
products immediately.

Moving forward, it seemed to me that my work with Tougaloo
was a logical extension of the token efforts I had made in the past—
within the company, during the Selma to Montgomery march the year
before, and in the church—to relate to the civil rights struggle. I had
come to believe that the race problem in America was the greatest
single moral, ethical, and religious dilemma facing us at that time.
Unless we could solve it, we were making a mockery of the democratic
and Christian heritage of the nation.

Someone once said that we do Christ a disservice if we preach the
gospel when bread is needed. To me, the "bread" the Negro needed in
the South was quality education. The gospel was preached in that area
of the country to overflowing, but as whites practiced Christianity,
they mocked the message of Jesus in the eyes of black people.
The preaching of the gospel was still needed in the South, to be sure,
but I thought we also needed to provide the "bread" of available
quality education. Tougaloo offered such an education. It was not the
whole answer to the problem, but I believed it was a step in the right
direction.

Chapter 33

The Best Birthday Present

As I once again sat behind a desk on April 1, 1966, it was with a sense of purpose and mission. Pressure was on me to accomplish a difficult task, but it was different from before. No longer did I have to get up every few minutes to gasp for breath. The crushing sensation in my chest had left me the night of our decision four months earlier. From that moment forward, I had no more trouble breathing.

In the weeks ahead, I planned programs, wrote letters, and conferred with numerous people about the campaign for Tougaloo. Simultaneously, Linda and I made final plans for our trip to Africa.

Late in June, just two weeks before we were to leave for Africa, I experienced another of God's miracles. I was sitting in my office late on a Friday afternoon. All of a sudden, the idea popped into my head to call my old friend, Eugene Gilbert, president of Gilbert Marketing Group. I had become good friends with him in 1963 while we worked together on the magazine *Off to College.* For three months in the fall of that year, I had an office at his company headquarters on 42nd Street in New York. I had not seen him in more than a year, and I had been thinking about giving him a call for several weeks. I wanted to tell him about Tougaloo. More important, I wanted to share with him the changes I had experienced in my life. Every time I had started to call Gene, I hesitated because I was not sure how he would react to what I had done. Would he laugh at me? Would he think I was crazy? I didn't know because I had never talked to Gene about my faith. He had casually mentioned to me in the past that he was not a religious man, so I had been careful not to pursue the subject.

This time, though, I had a strong feeling that I needed to call him. I looked at my watch. It was four-thirty. I thought, *I'll call and get an appointment for next week.*

I dialed his number. The receptionist answered and put me through to him. He recognized my voice immediately. "Where are you?" he asked.

"I'm here in New York."

"Come on over."

I protested momentarily, citing the lateness of the day and the fact that I was calling to set up a time to see him next week.

"Come on over now," he insisted. "I want to see you now."

I hung up the phone, called Linda to tell her I'd be late for supper, and dashed out to catch a subway to Gene's office on the east side of Manhattan.

As I rode over there, I practically felt my knees knocking. How would he react to what I planned to tell him? Gene was a great story-teller and jokester. One of his favorite greetings was, "Let me tell you a funny story." He and I had shared hundreds of "funny stories." We had partied together, laughed together, and worked together. I had said thousands of words to him, but not one about my faith. What would he think of me sitting there in his office talking seriously about God and my experiences of the past few weeks?

I did not have long to speculate about these questions because the subway ride to his office was only fifteen minutes.

Gene greeted me warmly when I walked into his office. Almost immediately he began asking questions about the business. "How are things going in the company? What's your latest project? Making lots of money? What brings you to New York?" My answers were general and vague. Then I said, "Gene, I want to share something with you."

He leaned forward to listen.

"I'm not with the company anymore," I began. "I left in November. A tremendous change has come into my life." For the next thirty minutes I told him about what I had experienced during the past four months. I told him of my faith in God and Christ and how I was convinced that God had led me into the decisions I had made.

I told him we had sold everything in Montgomery and given the money away.

Then I paused.

He had sat transfixed while I spoke. Now he leaned back and sighed.

"Millard," he said slowly, "you don't know what today is, do you?"

"No," I answered.

"Today is my fortieth birthday, and I want you to know that you have just given me the best birthday present of my life."

We both sat in silence for a few moments. Then he looked at his watch. "I've got to go now. I have an engagement tonight, but I want to give you a ride home so we can talk some more along the way." All the way to our apartment, he fired questions at me. The last thing he said before I left him that night was that he wanted to talk to me further, and he wanted me to talk to his wife.

In the days that followed, I spoke with him several times on the phone. One evening, Linda and I joined him and his wife for dinner. For hours that night we talked about faith, money, God and Christ, and, of course, Gene told a few "funny stories." An executive of the Ford Motor Company joined us for the meal. After Gene told my story as I had related it to him, this man said he thought what I did was senseless. Gene's wife, Nancy, commented that she was afraid he was going to give their money away! (Gene had already sent me a $500 check for Tougaloo.)

Gene was deeply affected by the story I had told him. He asked for my picture to hang in his office. I declined and told him not to give me credit for what happened in my life. From mutual friends, I learned that in the days following my visit, he told everyone he encountered the story I had shared with him.

Two weeks went by. Then, on the Sunday prior to our departure for Africa, as we entered the lobby of our residence hotel upon our return from church, the desk clerk called to me. "Mr. Fuller? Message."

I walked over. "Call Mrs. Gilbert" was scribbled on a note pad.

"What does she want?" I wondered.

We hurried upstairs and into our apartment. I dialed the number on the note. Someone answered, and I asked for Mrs. Gilbert. In the background I could hear voices.

In a moment, Nancy picked up the phone. She was crying.

"What's wrong?" I urgently asked.

"Millard," she half cried and half whispered, "could you please come over here? Gene died last night of a heart attack."

"Died? Gene is dead?"

"Yes," she whispered, "He's dead."

I couldn't believe it. What a shock!

He was in the bloom of youth. Only forty years old. Vigorous. Apparently full of health. Certainly the picture of health. And now he was dead.

I went to the apartment that afternoon. She was beside herself with grief, and she wanted me to explain what had happened to Gene during his last few weeks. She couldn't understand why he was so excited about my story. I talked with her reassuringly and gave her as much comfort as I could.

Surely the hand of God led me to my friend to share with him the way of salvation. You may see something different. To many, perhaps, the story is without meaning. But consider this episode in light of 1 Corinthians 1:21-25:

> For God in his wisdom made it impossible for men to know him by means of their own wisdom. Instead, God decided to save those who believe, by means of the "foolish" message we preach. Jews want miracles for proof and Greeks look for wisdom. As for us, we proclaim Christ on the cross, a message that is offensive to the Jews and nonsense to the Gentiles. This message is Christ who is the power of God and the wisdom of God. For what seems to be God's foolishness is wiser than man's wisdom. And what seems to be God's weakness is stronger than men's strength.

Chapter 34

Off to Africa

On July 1, Linda and I flew to Africa to fulfill our long-appointed destiny with that great continent. (My dad and stepmother had flown to New York a few days earlier to get the children and drive back to Alabama in our car.) For nearly two months, we lived through the most exciting and rewarding adventure of our lives.

Our travels carried us more than twenty thousand miles and into twelve countries—Senegal, Liberia, Nigeria, Uganda, Republic of Congo, Malawi, Kenya, Tanzania, Rhodesia [now Zimbabwe], Republic of South Africa, Democratic Republic of the Congo, and Ghana. We spent significant time traveling in the latter five. Along the way, we saw beautiful, modern cities and rode on super highways. We also visited remote villages that could only be reached by hiking narrow paths. We stayed one night in a plush hotel in Kenya and another in a straw hut in Congo. We traveled commercially by modern airplanes piloted primarily by Africans or Europeans as well as in a small private plane piloted by a missionary doctor. Runways were long and smooth at modern airports; otherwise, we landed on strips of grass carved from the dense jungle.

We took a 150-mile canoe trip up the Congo River. We witnessed traditional African singing and dancing in every country, but also heard an African choir present Handel's *Judas Maccabaeus*. We saw people wearing everything from flowing robes and beads to grass skirts, but on average more in Western dress. We conversed with dozens of Africans who spoke English to some degree or another and listened in wonder as countless others spoke to us in Swahili, Shona, Chendau, Zulu, Xhoxa, Lingala, Luncundu, Uncundu, Chokosi, Twi,

Ewe, Fanti, and other African languages. A man in upper Congo had teeth filed to sharp points.

In Ghana, we were guests one day of a former president of the United Nations, and on another day we visited with a justice of Ghana's Supreme Court. We saw hundreds of friendly faces and a few filled with hate. One night, on a lonely road in Congo, poker-faced Congolese soldiers aimed guns at us and our car and searched our luggage.

We saw thousands of wild animals in a South African game park. Linda filmed a movie of a pride of lions stalking and attacking some impala. We were invited to attend a wedding held outside because the church wasn't nearly large enough to hold everyone. During the trip, we ate typical foods one finds in that part of the world—locally grown tropical fruits, yams, and manioc and occasionally exotic fare such as crocodile, ostrich, and different kinds of fish. I helped deliver a baby. We watched helplessly as a young girl who had starved to death took her last breath. Some eight-year-olds already had grey hair and didn't have enough energy to play due to lack of nourishment. On the other hand, we also romped with sturdy, healthy children.

One evening, at a little river village in upper Congo, Linda almost burned up the little grass hut in which we stayed as she tried to fry fish over an open fire. Palm oil in the frying pan overheated, and flames leaped almost to the thatched roof. Quick action by a Congolese guide who was with us averted a tragedy. He grabbed the pan off the fire and dumped the flaming oil on the earthen floor. In a matter of seconds, the crisis ended, but the villagers were excited. All around us we heard anxious chattering interspersed with laughter. Doubtless, they were worried about what could have happened, and yet they saw the humor in "that white woman" not knowing how to cook.

Our primary task in Africa was to visit missionaries and see church work, and this aspect of our trip gave us our greatest joy. Starting in Tanzania in East Africa and ending with Ghana in West Africa, we saw the church at work.

In Tanzania, Rhodesia, the Republic of South Africa, and Ghana, we met more than fifty missionaries of the United Church of Christ. In Congo and South Africa, we visited more than twenty-five

Disciples of Christ missionaries, and all along the way we talked to scores of missionaries of the Catholic Church, Mennonite, the Unevangelized Fields Mission, Church World Service of the National Council of Churches, and Baptist, Lutheran, Methodist, Presbyterian, Anglican, and other denominations.

We found some of the missionaries living in the middle of modern cities in houses not much different from typical middle-class housing in America. Others lived in small towns, and some lived in remote areas out in the bush. Most lived in relative safety (in many places they were safer than in certain areas of the United States), but some lived in explosive and potentially volatile situations. Many enjoyed the benefits of modern living—electricity, radio, television, indoor toilets, hot water, and so forth—while others lived without these amenities. Clearly, there was a wide range of missionary lifestyles in Africa.

Chapter 35

Near and Far

In addition to the missionaries we met in our travels, we talked to dozens of African pastors and laymen in every country, and they shared with us their thoughts and ideas about the Christian presence in Africa.

The best-known layman we were privileged to meet was Chief Albert Luthuli, the famed Zulu Nobel Peace Prize winner and former leader of the African National Congress in South Africa. We spent more than two hours with this devout Christian layman at his little farm near Groutville.

At the time of our visit, he had been restricted by the government for twelve years to an area within a fifteen-mile radius from his home. The government forbade him to go to any meetings or even attend church. He was prohibited from writing about anything, and it was a crime for a person to quote him. Their suppression of Chief Luthuli stemmed from his open opposition to the system of apartheid in South Africa that separated the races and deprived all non-whites of any political, social, or economic rights.[1]

Chief Luthuli expressed his deep concern for his country. He longed for the day when black people would be treated equally, and he deplored the racial system that existed in South Africa. But he never expressed the slightest bitterness toward his white oppressors.

Near the end of our visit, I asked Chief Luthuli the following question: "If you had a microphone and could address the American people, what would you say to them about helping with South Africa's racial problems?"

The answer was quick to come, as if he had been thinking about such an opportunity. He rested an elbow on his knee and raised three

South Africa's Rainbow

The word "apartheid" literally means "separate." Prior to 1991, South African law defined four distinct groups of people in Africa: whites, blacks, "coloreds," and Indians (Asian Indians who came to South Africa in great numbers to build railroads). Though the law has since been abolished, many South Africans still define themselves and others according to these categories.

Whites were by far the privileged class from western cultures, mostly of Dutch decent who settled in South Africa much like Europeans who firmly established themselves in America during the seventeenth and eighteenth centuries. Through stringent rules and regulations and physical barriers, whites had their own neighborhoods, their public seating areas, their parks, their beaches, their train stations and coaches, rest rooms, water fountains, and on and on. Everything for whites was first class. "Coloreds" were considered a race mixture of black and white. I'm not sure this is true, but the locals told us they had the "pencil test" for distinguishing between black and "colored." When a pencil was inserted into one's hair, if it slid out, that person was documented as "colored." On the other hand, if it stuck, one was designated as black. It was preferable to be in the "colored" group because that status awarded one a few more privileges.

We learned that citizens of South Africa were strictly required to carry an identification card at all times. If a person worked for a white employee, even as a domestic in a home, he or she had to have a special permit to enter that area of town. Black, "colored," and Indian people who violated this law were jailed.

For Millard and me, who were raised in the Deep South, this higher level of racial prejudice we observed in South

Africa was shocking. In the U.S., we called it "segregation." In South Africa, it was called "apartheid." Of the two systems, "apartheid" was the more extreme.

—Linda Fuller

fingers. "I'd say three things," he intoned. "First, I'd advise them to eliminate the word 'Negro' from the American vocabulary. Have only 'black Americans' and 'white Americans' and grant equality in fact as well as in law to your black citizens. Second, I'd tell your American businesses which are bringing their money and machines to South Africa to bring along their Christian principles. Third, I'd say help us get as many black South Africans in American universities as possible."

At the end of our visit, Chief Luthuli led us in a prayer. We shook hands and left. A year later, we learned that he was killed by a train as he walked across a trestle, thus ending another sad chapter in South Africa's history.

One of the most famous ministers we met in Africa was a white man, Dr. Bayers Naude, a South African Dutch Reformed minister. Like Chief Luthuli, Dr. Naude became concerned with the race problem in South Africa and began to inform himself on the subject. He reread the New Testament in light of his findings and decided that, as a Christian, he could no longer support the government's policy of apartheid.

He began to preach against it from his pulpit. In short order, he was dismissed from his church. At that time, he organized the Christian Institute, an interracial body dedicated to informing white South Africans of the cruel practices of apartheid. Dr. Naude said that if the whites of South Africa understood how apartheid worked, they would oppose it. (The overwhelming majority of the white population of three and a half million in South Africa are Christian.[1])

Dr. Naude charted a dangerous course for himself in South Africa, but he understood the risks. He told me that he did not seek martyrdom, but that he was willing to pay that price if he must. His was a prophetic voice in a troubled land.

Another outstanding layman we met was Samuel Amissah, a Ghanaian who serves as general secretary of the All-Africa Conference of Churches, with headquarters in Nairobi, Kenya. We visited with him at his home in Winneba, Ghana, for most of one Sunday. We worshiped with him and his lovely wife at the Methodist church in Winneba, toured the town, went for a swim at the beach (one of the most beautiful we had ever seen), and ate a real feast at his home. Mainly, we talked about Africa, the Christian presence there, and especially the All-Africa Conference of Churches. Mr. Amissah was unquestionably one of the most articulate spokesmen for the church on the continent. We found him to be a charming man with insights into the role of Christianity in Africa and strong feelings about making the Christian presence more of a relevant and powerful force there.

He explained that for many years people felt that the church of Africa was started by missionaries from America or from Europe, and that the theology was, of course, slanted toward a Western interpretation and background. The thinking of Africans wasn't taken very seriously. But, as Africans had theological training, some began to be in charge of theological colleges or take roles as heads of departments of religious studies at universities.

We talked with many other pastors and laymen. All of them seemed anxious to build up the church and make it a force for good in their land. They recognized the many problems, but they saw the opportunities, too. We were encouraged by our fellowship with these Christian brothers and sisters, for we felt that we were working together—all a part of the same worldwide fellowship of believers, all members of Christ's church.

Throughout Africa, we found Christians worshiping, evangelizing, educating the unlearned, caring for prisoners, healing the sick, feeding the hungry, giving water to the thirsty, clothing the naked, and welcoming the stranger.

Our most dramatic encounter with evangelism was in Northern Ghana. Al Krass, a United Church of Christ missionary, had worked there among the people of the Chokosi tribe since 1964. Prior to his arrival, the language of the tribe had never been recorded. There were no books or writings in their native tongue. Before 1961, the gospel had never been preached to them. Al learned the language. He began to translate portions of the New Testament into Chokosi and teach the people how to read. He also began to preach. By the time of our arrival, with the aid of three Ghanaian evangelists, one from the South and two from the North, he had converted and baptized more than six hundred people into the Christian faith.

Al Krass was one of the most dedicated and effective Christians I had ever met. Converted in college from Jewish Agnosticism, Al took the command of the New Testament to "go and preach" as a personal directive. Christ and the Christian faith were real to him. He knew—through the before and after of his conversion experience—that the Christian faith gives meaning, purpose, and direction to life.

He lives in the small town of Chereponi with his wife, Sue, and their two small sons. The nearest white family is sixty miles away, and the nearest good hospital is more than one hundred miles away. They live without most modern conveniences. For six months out of the year, there is no precipitation in the area, and the temperature often gets unbearably hot. But when anyone asks Al and Sue if they are sacrificing anything to live there, their answer is a quick no. They believe God's call to service is a privilege, a joy—not a burden. We did not find a single missionary who saw himself or herself in a role of a "suffering servant." Without exception, they saw their work as an opportunity and privilege, not primarily as a responsibility.

We heard Al preach one Sunday during our stay with them. The little church with mud walls and floor was packed with people we had "recruited" from a nearby open-air market. Most had never heard of Jesus Christ. Al used the familiar text on love from 1 Corinthians 13. After reading the chapter, Al asked his congregation the question, "What is the most important thing in the world?"

Some said "happiness." Others said "money," "life," or "my house." A few said "wife" or "wives." Al wrote these things on a wall behind him. Then he talked about them. He concluded that all of them were indeed important. Finally, he turned to the wall again and wrote to the left of the list *Kolo*, the Chokosi word for love. Then, with this word as the center, he drew a cross. "God loves you," he said, speaking in Chokosi. "He sent his Son, Jesus." Al went on to tell, briefly and clearly, the story about Jesus' birth and what he did to show love to those he met. "Because God loves you," he continued, "he sent his Son to express this love. Because God loves you, love one another."

Sitting in that service was a soul-stirring experience for us. With goats peering in the door from time to time, a blind man and a leper sitting on the pew beside us, and dozens of eager eyes fastened upon the preacher, it could have been like what the first preachers of the gospel faced as they traveled around telling people about the good news of Christ.

The message was revolutionary among the people. Al told us there was an average of one death a month in the tribe from poisoning, with the average greatly increasing during their festival season in January and February. If you don't like your neighbor, poison him. That was the practice. And the poisonings were only one symptom of a wider condition of distrust and hostility toward neighbors. Al proclaimed a message of "loving your neighbor." What a difference!

In addition to evangelism and literacy work, Al Krass builds latrines, constructs dams, and attempts to relate to the physical needs of the people in other ways. His is an inspiring work, and we were greatly enriched for visiting with him, his family, and his new Christian friends among the Chokosis.

As if all these experiences weren't exciting enough, we had no idea of the drama that would unfold next.

Note

1. According to the U.S. State Department, the population of South Africa in 2010 is 49.3 million, comprising 39.4 million blacks and 4.5 million whites. The religion of South Africa is still predominantly Christian (U.S. Department of State, "Background Note: South Africa," Bureau of African Affairs, 15 June 2010, http://www.state.gov/r/pa/ei/bgn/2898.htm [accessed 11 July 2010]).

Chapter 36

Way-Out Adventures

During our visit to the Chikore Mission station in Rhodesia, Linda and I had an exciting adventure with Dr. Donaldson. We were there on a Saturday and Sunday. When we retired on Saturday night, we planned to attend worship services in the Chikore church the following morning, but at dawn we heard a rap on our door. It was Dr. Donaldson.

"I've got an emergency case out in the bush," he announced. "Would you like to come along?"

We said we would. Quickly, we dressed, ate half of a hastily prepared breakfast, grabbed the other half in our hands, jumped in a Land Rover, and bounced off down the road.

Dr. Donaldson told us about the case as we rode along an unbelievably rough road. A man had walked all night—a distance of nineteen miles across country—to fetch the doctor because a woman had been in labor for three days and still had not delivered her child. The woman, this man reported, was now in critical condition.

For more than two hours we bounced and lurched over the nineteen-mile distance that separated trained Christian compassion from a desperate need. Finally, we reached the clearing where the villagers had brought the woman down to the road.

She was lying on the ground with only a grass mat between her and the soil. A few blankets were thrown over her. A fire had been built nearby, but it had died down. It was cold that morning. Ashes had fallen in the woman's face and on the blankets. She writhed in pain but was too weak to make many sounds. She was small and looked to be in her early twenties. Many people stood around looking, undoubtedly wondering if she was going to live or die.

Dr. Donaldson went right to work. He examined her quickly and then inserted a needle in her arm through which she could receive glucose. Linda held the glucose bottle at first, but then she turned pale and started to faint, so I took it. In a few minutes, Dr. Donaldson was ready to load the woman into the Land Rover for the long and rough trip to the hospital.

The woman, we learned, was the youngest of three wives. Her husband and the eldest wife rode to the hospital with us. The older wife would help care for her at the hospital during her time of recovery.

Another two hours later, we arrived back at the hospital. We unloaded the woman and took her immediately to the delivery room. Two African nurses came to assist, and I stepped outside the door to await the outcome. In a few minutes, one of the nurses rushed to the door and asked me to come in. The woman had revived and was struggling. They needed help to keep her on the operating table.

Dr. Donaldson was having trouble maneuvering the baby through the birth canal. He had already determined that it was dead—and had been dead for some time. The head was large, he said, and that was why the woman could not give birth to the infant. Also, the woman was quite small, and this was her first pregnancy.

In order to get the baby, Dr. Donaldson had to use forceps to pull out the little lifeless form.

It was mid-afternoon before Dr. Donaldson finished working. When he finally came out of the operating room, he said the woman had a fifty-fifty chance of surviving, but he didn't have long to speculate on her condition. He had to see his other patients. Being the only doctor at a hospital is a full-time job. With an emergency case thrown in, it is even more of a job.

By evening, though, he was able to join a group of other missionaries and African personnel in his living room for a period of worship. We sang hymns of praise and prayed together, and the African superintendent of the churches delivered a meditation.

What a day! And what a way to end it! Our hearts were warmed beyond description at seeing firsthand one practicing the command of Jesus to heal the sick and minister to those in need. As I watched him that night singing the hymns in the worship service, my eyes filled with tears of joy, for I realized that Dr. Donaldson not only knew *how* to heal the sick, but he knew the deep meaning of *why* he was healing them.

The next morning, our first question was, "How is the young woman?" We were disheartened to learn that she had contracted pneumonia. Dr. Donaldson said she had suffered too much exposure lying out by the road on the damp earth. Her chances of survival looked slim. When we left Chikore later in the morning, we asked Dr. Donaldson to let us know how she faired. We expected to hear the worst, but two months later, after we were back in the States, we received a letter from him advising that she made a complete recovery and returned to her village in perfect health. We were overjoyed.

In Congo, in the northwest at Lotumbe, a Disciples missionary, Dr. John Ross, built a hospital and several clinics in outlying villages. We spent several days with him. He gave us a tour of the hospital at Lotumbe and the nearby Leprosy Mission supported by the American Leprosy Society, and also took us in his small plane to visit one of his village clinics.

Dr. Ross was one of the most remarkable men we had ever met. Until age thirty-six, he had served as a pastor. He and his wife had several children. One by one, for various reasons, all of them died. At such a time of sorrow and loss, it would have been easy to turn away from their faith. Rather, Dr. Ross felt God's call to return to college to become a physician. At age forty, he graduated from medical school. He volunteered for medical missionary service in the Congo. When we met him, he had been in Congo for sixteen years. On two successive furloughs to the United States during this period, he had learned to fly an airplane and trained in aviation mechanics. He preaches, practices medicine, flies his own airplane to outlying clinics, repairs the plane when it develops trouble, and often provides music in church by playing the accordion. His work in Congo was the subject of an award-winning television show titled "Monganga" (literally, "white doctor") in the *March of Medicine* series (NBC, November 1956).

Linda and I had the privilege of visiting with Dr. Keith Fleshman in Congo. I asked him why he thought the church needed to be involved in medical work.

He replied, "It is part of the social action of the church constrained to make loving acts of mercy rather than a sort of puffy feeling just left of the breastbone. As Jesus came 'that they might have life and have it more abundantly,' so the church attempts imitation on all levels, including the physical. . . . some folks accuse us of underhandedly using the 'bait' of medical aid as an 'evangelism trap.' This is not the primary intent. But when real love and concern for an individual provokes the question, 'Why?' and the answer of 'Why' provokes the question, 'Then why not I?' it is hard to feel guilty."

Linda and I departed from Africa near the end of August. Over these past seven weeks, we realized that we had witnessed the church at work. We found many problems along the path of our journey, but we literally bubbled inside about all the *good* things we saw servants of Christ doing in every country we visited.

Since returning to the United States, I have spoken extensively (more than one hundred times in the first year) from coast to coast about missionary work in Africa and about the incredible events that led us there. Nearly always, I conclude my programs with a reading from the twenty-fifth chapter of Matthew, which captures the spirit of missionary activity not only in Africa, but at home and around the world:

> You who are blessed by my Father, come! Come and receive the kingdom which has been prepared for you ever since the creation of the world. For I was hungry and you fed me, I was thirsty and you gave me drink; I was a stranger and you received me in your home; naked and you clothed me; I was sick and you took care of me; in prison and you visited me. The righteous will then answer him: "When, Lord, did we ever see you hungry and feed you, or thirsty and give you drink? When did we ever see you a stranger and welcome you in our home or naked and clothe you? The King will answer back, "I tell you, indeed, whenever you did this for one of these poorest brothers of mine, you did it for me!"

The Africa trip was more than an adventure for us. It was a fulfill-ment of destiny. I believe it was providential. In gathering material for this book, I looked up the letter I wrote to Jim Waery in 1964. The precise wording of that letter was, "It is possible that *by the summer of 1966* I will be in a position to devote the time necessary for such a program." In the middle of summer 1966, Linda and I were in the middle of our trip in the middle of Africa. But, had it not been for the dramatic events of late 1965, I would never have made the trip. Truly, "God moves in mysterious ways his wonders to perform."

Chapter 37

"Far beyond Our Strength"

We were on a new road, traveling in a new direction. We have the same God as before, but with an important difference—we now listen and obey as best we know how, and we depend upon the leading of God's Holy Spirit in our lives.

A friend once wrote to me at a time of crisis in her life. Her father was critically ill and expected to die at any moment. My friend was distraught. I wrote her a long letter in which I shared about my period of sadness, loneliness, and despair. I told her about the turmoil that came to Linda's and my marriage and how, in this desperate time of our lives, I began to realize that I was estranged not only from my wife and children, but also from my other fellow human beings and from God. Then I told her of the new philosophy and direction of our lives. Here is what I told her:

> Out of all this chaotic mess came a new direction in our lives. Loneliness and despair have given way to brighter and happier days. For weeks after we made our change, while intermittent sadness and happiness filled my heart, I sang or hummed over and over and over the old church hymn I had heard so often as a child, "We're Marching to Zion." What a joy and comfort I received from the stirring words and melody of that great old hymn! . . . .
>
> Life is either a soul-building process or it is merely a decaying process. Indeed, we are marching to Zion if we are about the business of soul building. But we march only toward the grave if we are not concerned with things of the spirit.

In these days of sadness, take comfort in the life your father has lived and the intangible gifts he has given to you and others who have known him. These things will live on, in you, and through you, in others.

Sing the song that means most to you. . . . Life ebbs and flows. We have loved ones with us for a while, and they are gone, but God is and ever has been and will ever be! We can set our anchor there. We can put our trust there, and we will never be disappointed!

I'll be thinking about you and praying with you in the days ahead.

Life has meaning for me now. People are again fellow human beings and not simply objects to be manipulated for self-serving purposes. The sun is a little brighter, the sky a little bluer, and the grass a little greener. Things make sense, and I see God's hand everywhere. I feel that I am going somewhere, not just running around in circles. I read the Bible with greater interest and understanding. Linda and I pray together frequently, something we never did before. We have serious discussions about God and Christ and the Holy Spirit and about how we feel led in various situations. One month, for example, our lease ran out in our little apartment in Montclair, New Jersey. Linda looked everywhere for another place to live. Finally, she prayed to God and asked him to be her real estate agent. The next day, she found an apartment a few miles away.

Worship is more meaningful. In the past, I fell asleep in church nearly every Sunday. Since the transformation, the experience of worship is alive to me now. It is a joy. Before, it was simply a responsibility and a burden.

Do I ever doubt that I made the right decision? Do I ever question God's leading? Yes, indeed. The forces of evil are never far from us in this life, and that is true whether we are trying to walk in his way or whether we are open allies of the devil. Occasionally, I am tempted to depart from the path God has chosen for me. I have times of sadness, and thoughts race through my mind. "You shouldn't have," I tell myself. I think about the life of ease I could live, not having to work or worry about making money for groceries, rent, clothing, or other necessities of life. I remember the depths to which Linda and I sunk, and a horrible desperation crawls through my mind, followed by deep regret. However, I know where these thoughts and feelings come from, and I say to God, "Here I am; I need your help." Then I am reminded of God's grace and love for me, even when I went astray.

God speaks in many ways. Often it is through a fellow believer. In April 1966 I was going through a tough time, so I wrote Clarence Jordan at Koinonia Farm. I told him about my good days but fretted over my bad ones and expressed dismay over my ever-recurring despair. His answer brought God's message. Here it is, in part:

Dear Millard: It is easy to understand how you would not be in a mood to write or do little else after the spiritual metamorphosis you went through. Nor am I surprised that you alternate between depression and joy. However, it is not God's grace that is sporadic but our apprehension and reception of it. Because this is common to all us humans. (Even our Lord Himself, in His hour of greatest desperation and loneliness, wondered if God had forsaken Him.) We must not lose heart when God's presence seems far from us.

Your coming to us was a challenge and inspiration, and we felt greatly refreshed by your honesty, your searching, and your openness to the will of God and your sensitivity to the things of the spirit. We thank God that you and Linda entered into our lives, although for such a short time. You blessed us in many, many ways and for this we shall never cease to be grateful.

It is a joy to know that you finally worked things through with Dees and that the door in that direction is closed. It was a gate of hell for you, and had you continued in it much longer you may have never responded to God's grace. Your response to the call you heard was indeed right, Millard, and I am glad that you have never doubted it. May you never do so. It would be as the lame man doubting the rightness of obeying the command to pick up his bed and walk. Or the blind man to go wash and receive his sight. But the evil one is not through with you yet on this matter, for he is not that easily diverted from his task of ensnaring you.

You seem to have made a very wise and spirit-led disposition of the devil's trinkets. So long as you disposed of it in love and faith, even though some of it may not be wisely used for God, you yourself will have made no error. Your heart is clean. What happens after that is on the conscience of others. When the business man, Zacchaeus, decided to dispose of his wealth, he may not have found the proper poor on whom to bestow it, but said the Lord, "Today hath salvation come to *this* house!" That is how I feel in your case.

My concern for you now, Millard, is not what has happened in the past but what direction your life will take from here on out. . . .

We feel so inadequate to the tasks which we see stretching before us. Surely our vision exceeds our grasp and our opportunities go far beyond our strength. But I suppose the good Lord looks not to the size of our accomplishments but to the faithfulness of our hearts.

> In His love,
> Clarence

What of the future? The future is something I cannot predict. No longer do I live a planned life. I have found that a planned life is a frustrated life because there are endless crisis along the way that have the potential of wrecking the plan. One who lives a planned life lives in constant fear, even terror, that his plan will not be fulfilled. Indeed, "a planned life can only be endured" and suffered through! My task is to remain faithful to God and to be obedient to his will. I will go where I feel God is leading.

There are many possibilities: (1) missionary service—as an administrator of a relief program or hospital in some foreign country or a fundraiser in the United States for overseas church work; (2) the ministry—I would expect to obtain a seminary education in this eventuality; (3) lawyer—working with a national instrumentality of the church as a real estate advisor, etc., or going back into private (law) practice; (4) business—there is a great need in our world today for the church to involve itself in the economic well-being of developing peoples. Traditionally, the church abroad has had a preaching, teaching, and healing ministry. Perhaps I will work with the church on such a program.

Also, I must not discount the possibility of going back into business in the United States. As I have stated elsewhere, neither business nor the American free enterprise system is evil in and of itself.

Quite to the contrary, I am a strong supporter of business and free enterprise, but I know it is easy for a man in business to sell out his principles and compromise his faith for more profit.

As a Christian in business, or in anything else, one must be willing to place *everything* in some order of precedence behind service to God. You cannot serve God and business, or God and profits, or God and wealth. You can serve God and use these things, but when the order of precedence is reversed, trouble is sure to come. I reversed the order, and the consequences were near tragic. To get things back in focus, I had to start over. I seriously doubt that I will ever return to a career in business, but I cannot completely discount the possibility. To do so would make a mockery of my vowed intent to go *anywhere* that God leads me.

My present feeling is that God has called me—and continues to call me—into a service of direct involvement with building the kingdom of God on earth.

Upon returning from Africa, I resumed my work with Tougaloo College. For the present, at least, if not for a long time to come, I feel this is where I ought to be. I see the work as a direct extension of the church's ministry to the world and the needs of people.

I continue to speak widely about the needs of Tougaloo College, about overseas missions, and about the miracles of faith I have witnessed in my own life.

There are those who will say that what I did was foolish. But as each new day passes, I feel more confident of God's leading. Linda and I are close now. I know and love my children as never before. Our third child, Linda Faith, was born in May 1967. We have made more real friends since November 1965 than in the previous six years. With the obsessive albatross of moneymaking and other false gods gone, we know God as a living reality.

My purpose in life is to *live today* to the fullest, walking to the best of my ability in the footsteps of Christ, not living with a reckless abandon about tomorrow, next week, and next year, but also not being so focused on the future that I miss today.

Eight years after this book was completed, Millard and Linda Fuller founded Habitat for Humanity International. Under Millard's leadership, Habitat grew to become the world's largest nonprofit home builder. Millard's second book, *Bokotola* (1977), recounts the excitement and drama of the next phase of their remarkable journey: moving to Koinonia in 1968 to start industry, farming, and housing ministries with Clarence Jordan; living in Africa for three years to test the housing ministry concept and dealing with one adventure after the next; then launching Habitat for Humanity International in 1976.

Millard wrote eleven books before God called him home in 2009:

Beyond the American Dream (1968)
Bokotola (1977)
Love in the Mortar Joints (1980)
No More Shacks! (1986)
The Excitement Is Building (1990)
Theology of the Hammer (1994)
A Simple, Decent Place to Live (1995)
More Than Houses (2000)
Building Materials for Life, Vol. I (2002)
Building Materials for Life, Vol. II (2004)
Building Materials for Life, Vol. III (2007)

In addition, *The House that Love Built* (2007) by Bettie Youngs provides a comprehensive overview of the Fullers's lives, including their dramatic and controversial departure from Habitat for Humanity in 2005 and launch of The Fuller Center for Housing.

Visit *www.fullercenter.org/history* for a full history timeline.

1966—Millard at Kennedy International
airport checking in for 6-week trip to
5 countries in Africa to visit
missionary work.

Linda and Millard wave just as they are
boarding their flight to Africa.

Fall 1965—Daniel
Offiong, student
from Nigeria.

1966—Millard
snaps a photo of
Linda deplaning
in Johannesburg,
South Africa.

Typical African mud block and
thatched roof house.

Missionary Al Krass baptizing new
convert.

1966—Millard in
South Africa.

Village Chief with
some of his children.

Millard goes with missionary Dr. Stetson
to make a house call.

1966—Making friends in Congo,
Brazzaville

Millard tries on
native clothing for
men in Congo.

1966—Ghana

Linda in Congo
filming typical river
view.

Fishing village on coast near
Accra, Ghana

Strolling along Ghana shore.

Segregated township in South Africa

Mosquito net over bed—dwellings in this
village have no walls. Linda & Millard
learn that privacy is a luxury.

Linda takes a turn at
paddling up the
Lobenge Channel
clogged with water
hycinths.

Pirogues are main transportation in
Congo.

Washing clothes along the Congo River

Loading woman in labor into Land Rover to
transport her miles away to mission hospital.

Typical open market featuring plantain,
banana, pineapple, manioc, corn, palm nuts,
fresh and smoked fish, dried beans and rice.

Bosobele Mission—view from Dr. Ross'
single engine plane.

Dr. John Ross and his
airplane.

Millard interviewing Dr. Ross with a tape
recorder, getting tour of Lotumbe.

1967—Millard helps Chris and Kim with
their snow sledding in Montclair, NJ

1968–1971 Koinonia Farm—Fullers lived in
upstairs portion of 2-story building.

1968—Millard, Linda Chris, Kim, and Faith (14 months).

1970—Millard speaking at Koinonia worship service

May 1971—Millard Fuller at Koinonia.
Habitat for Humanity grows out of Koinonia soil.

Afterword

By Tony Campolo

It was more than twenty-five years ago (in the mid-1980s) that I got a telephone call from Millard Fuller. He said he wanted me to be on the board of Habitat for Humanity. I had never heard of Habitat. He told me all about it. I said, "And what are you going to do?" He said, "We are going to build houses for poor people."

"That sounds wonderful," I said. "Anything else?"

"Yeah, we are going sell houses to these people with no down payment, long-term mortgages, and no interest from the mortgages because the Bible says you shouldn't charge interest on poor people."

"That's great. And the money?"

"We are going to raise money for building supplies."

"Who is going to build these houses?"

"Church people."

I thought to myself, *He's crazy if he thinks congregations are going to build houses!*

Well, twenty-five years later, 300,000 houses have been built, and one and half million people are living in those houses—a lot of them built by churches!

People talk about changing political, social, and economic systems with grandiose ideas of making those changes from the top down. They talk about helping manufacturers of vehicles. They talk about helping the banks. They talk about helping the great institutions of society so that the benefits will trickle down.

Millard Fuller never believed in the trickle-down theory. He believed in the trickle-*up* theory. That's how this housing ministry was born. It started with a single house in rural Georgia. I believe that's how God's work grows, and that's how a grassroots movement changes the world—from the bottom up.

Millard was a dear friend. We first became acquainted at large gatherings where both of us were speakers. Our friendship grew through the years, and our wives became close friends, too. Both

Millard and I traveled almost constantly to and from speaking engagements, and our paths crossed from time to time. These serendipitous moments allowed time for us to talk and share what was going on in our lives and ministries. I knew Millard to be a deeply committed Christian motivated by the spirit of Christ working in and through him. Besides being a true man of God, he loved and spent significant time with his wife, children, and grandchildren.

Millard understood the Sermon on the Mount, and he lived by it. He believed in seeking the kingdom of God and his righteousness first and not worrying about things for himself. He wasn't anything like that guy Jesus talked about in the Bible—the one who filled his barn with stuff, thought to himself, *I'd better tear down this barn and build a bigger barn*, and then went and did it. That guy thought he had enough for security in his old age and figured it was time to retire and take it easy. He retired, thinking the money would carry him through, and the Lord said, "Thou fool!"

Millard didn't store anything up. In fact, he gave all his wealth away to the poor. This is exactly what God is still calling us to do. Neither did Millard believe in retirement because, according to him, the word "retirement" doesn't exist in the Bible. Millard told me that as long as he was able, strong both in body and mind, he wanted to continue with God's calling on his life.

Millard Fuller did what the rich young ruler in the tenth chapter of Mark declined to do. You remember the story of the young man who lived a good life and obeyed God's commandments. Jesus loved him but told him that he needed to sell everything he had, give the money to the poor, and follow him. The young man went away sad because he didn't want to give up his abundant possessions.

I think most of us are people like that rich, young ruler, and have great possessions. The good news is that Millard Fuller was also like that rich, young ruler in every respect. He was a good man, but he went beyond and did what the rich, young ruler failed to do. He gave away his wealth. He gave it away to follow Jesus. Jesus put it on Millard's heart to give to the poor and take care of the needy.

Millard once told me a story about a man who loved greyhound dogs. He rescued them from the racetracks to keep them from being euthanized when their racing days ended. A friend went to see the man who loved these greyhound dogs. There in the man's living room was one of the dogs, playing and rolling around with the man's children. They were having a good time together. Then the visitor looked right at the dog and said, "Dog, why aren't you racing anymore? Had you stopped winning?"

The dog replied, "No, I kept on winning."

"Well, then why did you quit? Weren't you making enough money for your owner?"

"Yes, I was making big money for the owner."

"Then why did you quit?" the man asked.

"Because one day I realized that rabbit I was chasing wasn't real."

How many of us end up in life chasing rabbits that aren't real?

Millard woke up one day and realized he was "chasing a rabbit" that wasn't real.

A millionaire at twenty-nine years of age, he was chasing a rabbit that most of us love to chase. He caught it, realized it wasn't real, and chose to give himself to what *is* real. He actually believed that if he sought God's kingdom and his righteousness first, then other things would take care of themselves!

Millard's life incarnated God's vision for all of us. For the thousands who knew him, we know how he effectively encouraged and challenged others in the numerous letters he dictated daily; the books he authored; the speeches he made; and the countless one-on-one conversations he had. Millard's vision came out of the sixty-fifth chapter of Isaiah, where the Prophet Isaiah describes the kingdom of God that's supposed to come when God's will is done on earth as it is in heaven. He tells of places where children do not die in infancy; where old people live out their lives in health and well-being; where everyone has a job; and where people *build houses and get to live in them themselves!* That's what Habitat for Humanity and now The Fuller Center for Housing are about—building houses and having people live in them.

God's people working together builds unity. That is what Millard called the "theology of the hammer." He wrote a book by that title (Smyth & Helwys, 1994). He was about bringing people together using the simple tools that the carpenter Jesus once used in a small town called Nazareth. Some theologies separate people, but the theology of the hammer brings people together. I have seen this theology lived out. I've been part of builds when I've seen Presbyterians, Roman Catholics, and Baptists all working together side by side! When diverse people start working together, you *know* it's the kingdom of God. They forget their theological differences because the Holy Spirit comes upon them when they put Christ's love into action. That's Christianity at its best—bringing people together as they give needy people a hand up.

Millard knew that what people did would change them. It's a concept in sociology called "praxis." What people do changes the way they think and the way they feel.

I was in Northern Ireland speaking at a series of evangelistic services that brought Catholics and Protestants together. At that time, it was unusual for them to be under the same roof. A young man came forward at the end of one of those meetings and gave his life to Christ. When I talked to him afterward, he said, "I don't know what to do. I'm probably going to have to quit the IRA." And then he said five times in a row, "I'm a terrorist. If I leave the Irish Republican Army, they'll kill me thinking that I might give away their secrets. I don't know what to do."

I called Millard. Millard said, "Well, I know what to do. Send him over to Americus, Georgia, and we'll put him to work for Habitat for Humanity."

This young man had the spirit of the antichrist when I met him. Two years later, he was transformed by working for the people of God. Millard knew that one could be changed while working for the poor and the oppressed.

When Jesus told the rich young ruler to sell what he had and give it to the poor, it wasn't simply because the poor needed help, but because Jesus knew what would happen to the man in the process of giving to the poor. That's exactly what happened to this young man from Ireland. Millard wanted his vision of "No More Shacks" to permeate both young and old.

The story gets even better. The young man from Ireland became an Anglican priest. He's back in his homeland preaching the gospel, bringing good news.

The Bible says the people perish. You don't have to be dead to be dead. If you don't have any vision for putting God's love into action, you are spiritually dead. Visions and dreams are what Habitat for Humanity and the Fuller Center for Housing offer today—an opportunity to live out a vision and to keep Millard's dream alive.

Linda told me that soon after Millard died on February 3, 2009, she was going through his billfold and found a small piece of paper tucked in a corner. It was a letter from a six-year-old boy that read, "Dear Mr. Millard, Thanks for writing me. You are a fine man. You are very nice, friendly, and kind. Give your wife a big hug from me. You are doing very well with this new Fuller Center. Someday I'll help you out. Your true friend, Lamari Tarver." That's a six-year-old kid with a vision! He's going to build houses someday because God has given him the vision through his relationship with Millard.

Millard could inspire people to do things they never imagined and then patted them on the back when they did them. I heard someone sum him up pretty well when he said, "He could talk a bulldog off of a meat wagon." Humorous but probably true.

Millard had a great capacity for attracting people of talent. It was almost uncanny how just the right person showed up at just the right time when something specifically unusual needed to be done. Millard called those coincidences "God's Incidences."

The one thing that Millard was good at, perhaps better than anybody else I knew, was getting donations. He knew how to extract money out of people's pockets and their bank accounts. He wanted givers to be blessed through acts of generosity just as the receivers of the good houses that the money helped build are blessed to have a decent place to live.

This book, *Beyond the American Dream*, covers the first thirty years of Millard's life. Many people know, as Paul Harvey would say, "the rest of the story," but few know much about what made Millard the man he became. It seems his first thirty years were simply laying a firm foundation for the next forty-four he unknowingly had left. The same drive and focus Millard had for producing an overabundance of wealth for himself were used to find resources to provide decent affordable homes for low-income families.

I love Peter, Paul, and Mary's song, "If I Had a Hammer." I think it is appropriate for moving forward in carrying on Millard's work of eliminating poverty housing. Here's how I'd like to word the song:

> If you have a hammer, you should hammer in the morning.
> You should hammer in the evening all over this world.
> You should hammer out freedom.
> You should hammer out justice.
> You should hammer out love between your brothers and your sisters
> all over this world.

In the name of Jesus and to the glory of God, hammer out freedom; hammer out justice; hammer out love; and in the name of Jesus, I say, Oyée, brother! Oyée, sister! Oyée, Millard.